Name : ___________

Subtraction Worksheets

| 6 | 13 | 6 |
| - 3 | - 1 | - 1 |

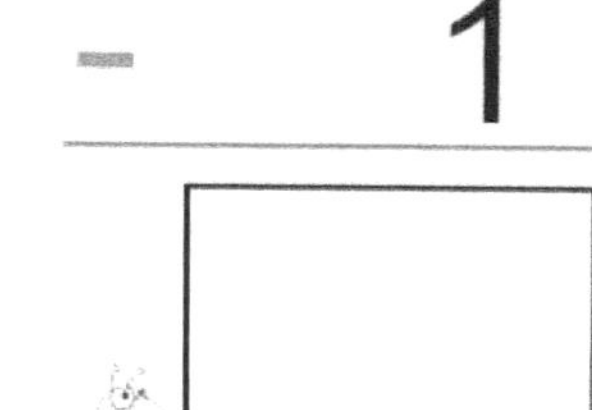

| 7 | 2 | 3 |
| - 4 | - 1 | - 2 |

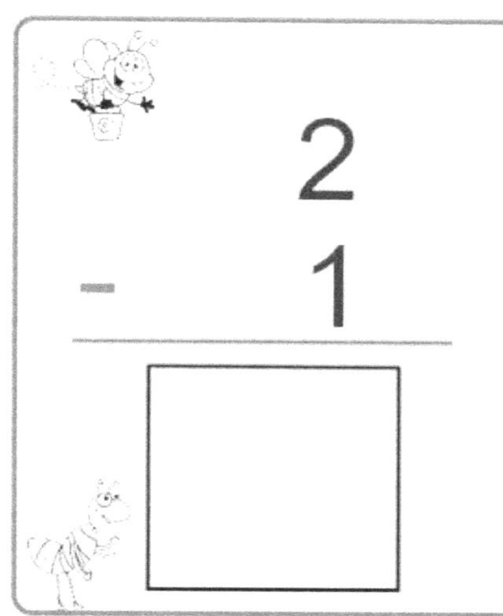
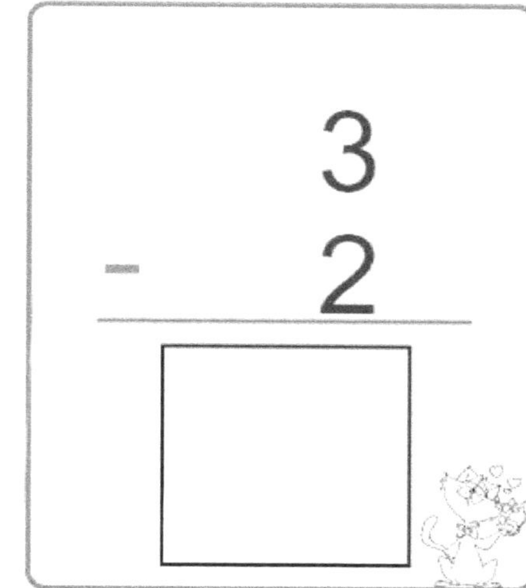

| 20 | 11 | 13 |
| - 13 | - 4 | - 9 |

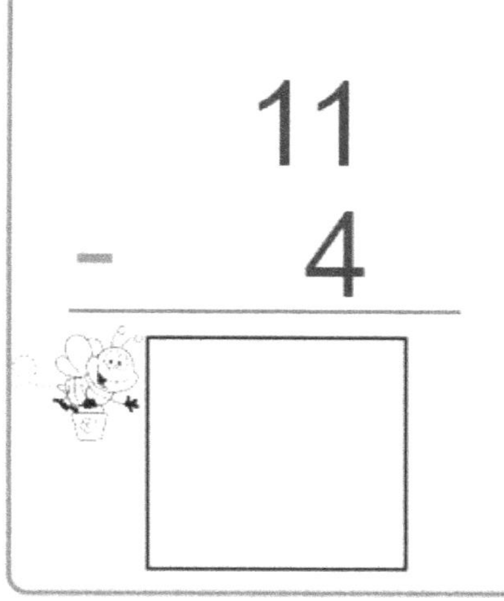
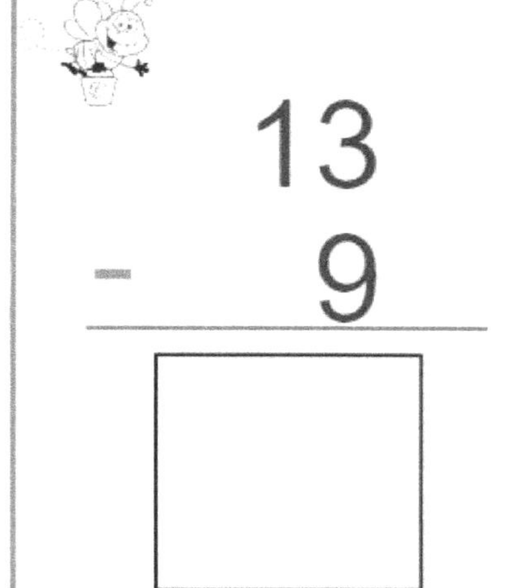

 Math Made Easy.... 

Name : _______________________

Direction: Use the picture to help you find the answer.

1 2 3 4 5 6 7 8 9 10

12 - 10 = _____

6 - 5 = _____

6 - 3 = _____

7 - 2 = _____

20 - 8 = _____

10 - 6 = _____

2 - 1 = _____

10 - 4 = _____

12 - 1 = _____

15 - 8 = _____

Name : _______________

Subtraction Worksheets

4 − 3	9 − 7	1 − 1
18 − 12	3 − 1	2 − 1
12 − 7	5 − 2	15 − 14

 Math Made Easy…. 

Name : _______________________

Direction: Use the picture to help you find the answer.

6 − 4 = ____

6 − 1 = ____

16 − 13 = ____

19 − 7 = ____

7 − 3 = ____

19 − 18 = ____

11 − 8 = ____

17 − 3 = ____

6 − 2 = ____

17 − 8 = ____

Subtraction Worksheets

7	17	3
− 1	− 2	− 2
☐	☐	☐

18	16	5
− 2	− 4	− 3
☐	☐	☐

18	18	20
− 16	− 17	− 16
☐	☐	☐

Math Made Easy....

Name : _______________________________

Direction: Use the picture to help you find the answer.

| 1 | 2 | 3 | 4 | 5 | 6 | 7 | 8 | 9 | 10 |

6 - 5 = ____

11 - 5 = ____

2 - 1 = ____

4 - 2 = ____

9 - 8 = ____

17 - 13 = ____

5 - 1 = ____

15 - 12 = ____

10 - 9 = ____

1 - 1 = ____

Subtraction Worksheets

8 − 4	6 − 4	15 − 4
2 − 1	17 − 9	18 − 11
17 − 2	8 − 5	18 − 11

Direction: Use the picture to help you find the answer.

16 - 1 =

11 - 4 =

19 - 9 =

2 - 1 =

10 - 9 =

13 - 4 =

16 - 11 =

2 - 1 =

5 - 2 =

20 - 1 =

Subtraction Worksheets

Name : __________________

7 − 1	18 − 15	5 − 3
7 − 2	4 − 2	5 − 2
10 − 3	17 − 7	1 − 1

Math Made Easy....

Name : _______________________

Direction: Use the picture to help you find the answer.

1 2 3 4 5 6 7 8 9 10

11 - 3 = ______

15 - 7 = ______

13 - 12 = ______

4 - 2 = ______

18 - 13 = ______

6 - 1 = ______

6 - 1 = ______

2 - 1 = ______

5 - 2 = ______

1 - 1 = ______

Subtraction Worksheets

11 − 6	18 − 14	11 − 5
18 − 17	16 − 7	8 − 2
19 − 1	5 − 1	18 − 7

Direction: Use the picture to help you find the answer.

1   2   3   4   5   6   7   8   9   10

7 - 1 = ___

20 - 2 = ___

8 - 2 = ___

17 - 9 = ___

1 - 1 = ___

12 - 6 = ___

1 - 1 = ___

17 - 12 = ___

5 - 2 = ___

7 - 5 = ___

Subtraction Worksheets

12 − 1	18 − 4	7 − 4
10 − 1	9 − 5	14 − 3
6 − 2	11 − 8	14 − 8

Name : ___________________________

Direction: Use the picture to help you find the answer.

1 2 3 4 5 6 7 8 9 10

4 − 2 = ___	8 − 3 = ___
16 − 2 = ___	16 − 15 = ___
14 − 12 = ___	8 − 3 = ___
18 − 3 = ___	20 − 6 = ___
8 − 6 = ___	3 − 1 = ___

Subtraction Worksheets

4 − 3	3 − 2	6 − 2
12 − 2	19 − 14	6 − 1
3 − 2	16 − 1	14 − 4

Direction: Use the picture to help you find the answer.

1   2   3   4   5   6   7   8   9   10

10 - 6 = ___

14 - 4 = ___

5 - 2 = ___

1 - 1 = ___

8 - 1 = ___

4 - 1 = ___

15 - 9 = ___

5 - 3 = ___

19 - 1 = ___

18 - 14 = ___

Name : _______________

Subtraction Worksheets

5 − 1	1 − 1	3 − 1
16 − 10	13 − 2	19 − 3
5 − 3	10 − 6	4 − 1

Math Made Easy....

Direction: Use the picture to help you find the answer.

13 − 3 = ____	19 − 17 = ____
14 − 1 = ____	8 − 4 = ____
2 − 1 = ____	7 − 6 = ____
9 − 6 = ____	19 − 10 = ____
6 − 3 = ____	13 − 7 = ____

Subtraction Worksheets

13	15	16
− 11	− 14	− 3

14	1	19
− 6	− 1	− 4

19	11	7
− 13	− 10	− 2

  Math Made Easy....

Direction: Use the picture to help you find the answer.

1   2   3   4   5   6   7   8   9   10

9 - 8 =

20 - 18 =

20 - 16 =

1 - 1 =

14 - 5 =

14 - 1 =

20 - 11 =

1 - 1 =

15 - 3 =

2 - 1 =

Name : _______________________

Subtraction Worksheets

7 − 5	8 − 5	13 − 3
17 − 5	3 − 1	18 − 13
18 − 14	19 − 11	12 − 7

Math Made Easy....

Direction: Use the picture to help you find the answer.

1 2 3 4 5 6 7 8 9 10

10 - 9 _____

14 - 1 _____

3 - 2 _____

14 - 6 _____

17 - 7 _____

4 - 2 _____

13 - 9 _____

7 - 1 _____

17 - 16 _____

14 - 4 _____

Subtraction Worksheets

1 − 1	20 − 3	15 − 10
8 − 4	6 − 1	3 − 1
19 − 18	11 − 7	4 − 2

Direction: Use the picture to help you find the answer.

1   2   3   4   5   6   7   8   9   10

11 – 2 = ___	6 – 1 = ___
2 – 1 = ___	12 – 3 = ___
1 – 1 = ___	12 – 2 = ___
11 – 6 = ___	15 – 11 = ___
3 – 2 = ___	2 – 1 = ___

Subtraction Worksheets

17 − 2	5 − 1	18 − 12
12 − 2	19 − 11	4 − 1
11 − 4	4 − 1	1 − 1

Direction: Use the picture to help you find the answer.

7 - 5 =	5 - 1 =
10 - 9 =	14 - 7 =
2 - 1 =	7 - 3 =
1 - 1 =	11 - 5 =
14 - 5 =	10 - 5 =

Subtraction Worksheets

14 − 10	12 − 6	6 − 5
13 − 6	14 − 4	17 − 1
11 − 7	19 − 11	7 − 2

Name : _______________________________

Direction: Use the picture to help you find the answer.

1 2 3 4 5 6 7 8 9 10

19 - 6 = ____

11 - 7 = ____

13 - 4 = ____

18 - 6 = ____

10 - 9 = ____

3 - 2 = ____

6 - 4 = ____

14 - 12 = ____

2 - 1 = ____

4 - 2 = ____

Subtraction Worksheets

11 − 2	17 − 10

11
− 2

15
− 14

13
− 10

14
− 2

16
− 4

8
− 4

8
− 1

Name : __________________________

Direction: Use the picture to help you find the answer.

1   2   3   4   5   6   7   8   9   10

7 − 3 = ___	20 − 19 = ___
19 − 6 = ___	16 − 14 = ___
3 − 2 = ___	9 − 4 = ___
16 − 9 = ___	11 − 8 = ___
7 − 1 = ___	19 − 1 = ___

Subtraction Worksheets

10 − 6	20 − 12	6 − 3
15 − 9	5 − 2	3 − 2
16 − 15	8 − 5	10 − 4

Name : _______________________

Direction: Use the picture to help you find the answer.

1   2   3   4   5   6   7   8   9   10

20 - 13 =

1 - 1 =

1 - 1 =

18 - 5 =

14 - 9 =

4 - 2 =

17 - 16 =

12 - 1 =

16 - 11 =

20 - 15 =

Subtraction Worksheets

20 − 15	18 − 6	2 − 1
4 − 2	2 − 1	6 − 3
10 − 1	3 − 2	16 − 12

11 − 4 = _____

12 − 2 = _____

13 − 1 = _____

8 − 4 = _____

8 − 4 = _____

2 − 1 = _____

18 − 15 = _____

17 − 15 = _____

16 − 10 = _____

19 − 11 = _____

20 − 6	11 − 7	18 − 10
5 − 4	20 − 18	3 − 1
13 − 12	4 − 2	9 − 8

1 2 3 4 5 6 7 8 9 10

4 - 2 = ___

16 - 13 = ___

15 - 10 = ___

11 - 7 = ___

18 - 9 = ___

5 - 2 = ___

1 - 1 = ___

15 - 13 = ___

8 - 1 = ___

9 - 3 = ___

Name : _______________

Subtraction Worksheets

14 − 4	10 − 4	1 − 1
2 − 1	5 − 3	19 − 1
13 − 6	16 − 1	7 − 1

Name : _______________________________

Direction: Use the picture to help you find the answer.

| 1 | 2 | 3 | 4 | 5 | 6 | 7 | 8 | 9 | 10 |

$7 - 3 =$ _____

$12 - 6 =$ _____

$3 - 1 =$ _____

$19 - 5 =$ _____

$6 - 5 =$ _____

$1 - 1 =$ _____

$6 - 4 =$ _____

$7 - 4 =$ _____

$9 - 6 =$ _____

$4 - 3 =$ _____

9 − 8 = ☐	16 − 14 = ☐	18 − 2 = ☐
10 − 1 = ☐	2 − 1 = ☐	11 − 10 = ☐
10 − 3 = ☐	7 − 2 = ☐	2 − 1 = ☐

Name : _______________________________

Direction: Use the picture to help you find the answer.

19 − 11 = ____	6 − 4 = ____
5 − 2 = ____	7 − 1 = ____
1 − 1 = ____	19 − 18 = ____
11 − 9 = ____	6 − 3 = ____
7 − 5 = ____	1 − 1 = ____

Subtraction Worksheets

16 − 5 ☐	3 − 1 ☐	8 − 4 ☐
4 − 2 ☐	16 − 13 ☐	17 − 1 ☐
7 − 1 ☐	19 − 1 ☐	7 − 2 ☐

Name : ________________________

Direction: Use the picture to help you find the answer.

1   2   3   4   5   6   7   8   9   10

3 - 1 = ___	6 - 5 = ___
15 - 9 = ___	11 - 9 = ___
10 - 7 = ___	15 - 7 = ___
17 - 4 = ___	19 - 13 = ___
10 - 3 = ___	20 - 8 = ___

Subtraction Worksheets

16 - 8 = ___	20 - 8 = ___
20 - 5 = ___	10 - 4 = ___
12 - 5 = ___	13 - 9 = ___
10 - 4 = ___	9 - 3 = ___
14 - 1 = ___	19 - 1 = ___

Subtraction Worksheets

20
− 11

2
− 1

18
− 12

16
− 14

19
− 6

20
− 12

8
− 4

16
− 8

9
− 3

Name : ___________________________

Direction: Use the picture to help you find the answer.

1   2   3   4   5   6   7   8   9   10

$2 - 1 = $ ____

$11 - 4 = $ ____

$18 - 14 = $ ____

$3 - 2 = $ ____

$13 - 10 = $ ____

$6 - 2 = $ ____

$3 - 2 = $ ____

$2 - 1 = $ ____

$5 - 2 = $ ____

$18 - 7 = $ ____

Subtraction Worksheets

Name : ___________

20 − 16	8 − 2	13 − 11
1 − 1	9 − 4	5 − 3
6 − 5	1 − 1	1 − 1

Math Made Easy....

Name : _______________________________

Direction: Use the picture to help you find the answer.

| 1 | 2 | 3 | 4 | 5 | 6 | 7 | 8 | 9 | 10 |

13 - 4 =

20 - 14 =

5 - 3 =

7 - 6 =

14 - 11 =

16 - 1 =

3 - 2 =

9 - 6 =

16 - 5 =

12 - 9 =

Subtraction Worksheets

19 − 18	20 − 11	16 − 6
13 − 6	4 − 1	2 − 1
8 − 4	20 − 15	14 − 2

Name : ________________

Direction: Use the picture to help you find the answer.

1   2   3   4   5   6   7   8   9   10

7 − 3 = ___	20 − 5 = ___
9 − 4 = ___	11 − 8 = ___
17 − 1 = ___	16 − 11 = ___
12 − 4 = ___	18 − 2 = ___
18 − 12 = ___	6 − 2 = ___

Subtraction Worksheets

13 − 10	19 − 14	3 − 2
2 − 1	2 − 1	8 − 3
19 − 9	15 − 7	11 − 2

Name : _______________________

Addition Worksheets

6 + 7	8 + 8	10 + 6
10 + 5	11 + 19	11 + 12
7 + 7	6 + 4	6 + 9

Math Made Easy....

Addition Worksheets

6 + 7	8 + 8	10 + 6
10 + 5	11 + 19	11 + 12
7 + 7	6 + 4	6 + 9

Name : _______________________

Direction: Add the number of images in each box and write the answer in the last box.

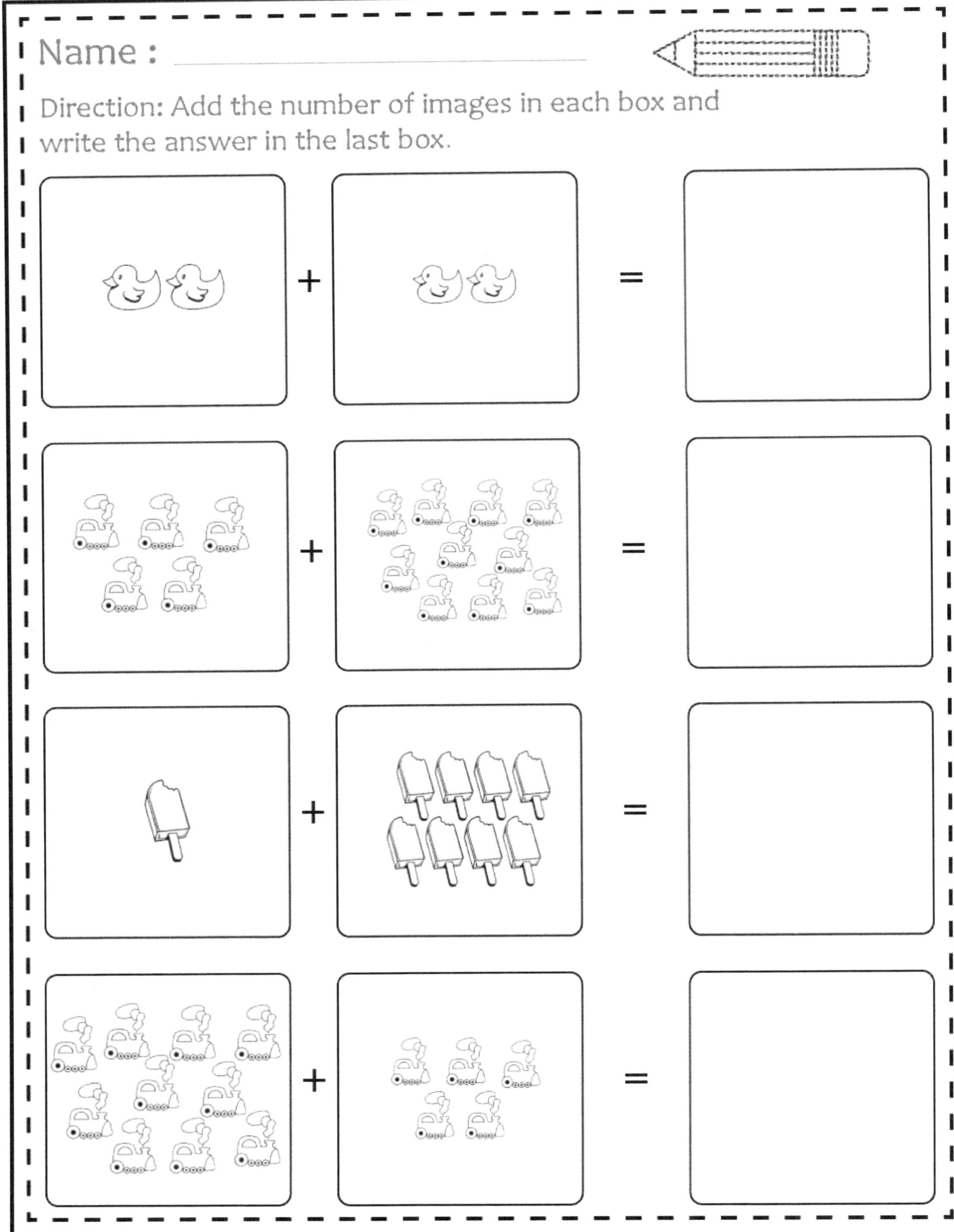

Addition Worksheets

3
+ 10

Answer

1
+ 3

Answer

3
+ 7

Answer

4
+ 8

Answer

3
+ 9

Answer

2
+ 10

Answer

Addition Worksheets

20 + 5	6 + 15	13 + 7
15 + 20	7 + 2	4 + 10
5 + 12	16 + 3	17 + 5

Name :

Direction: Add the number of images in each box and write the answer in the last box.

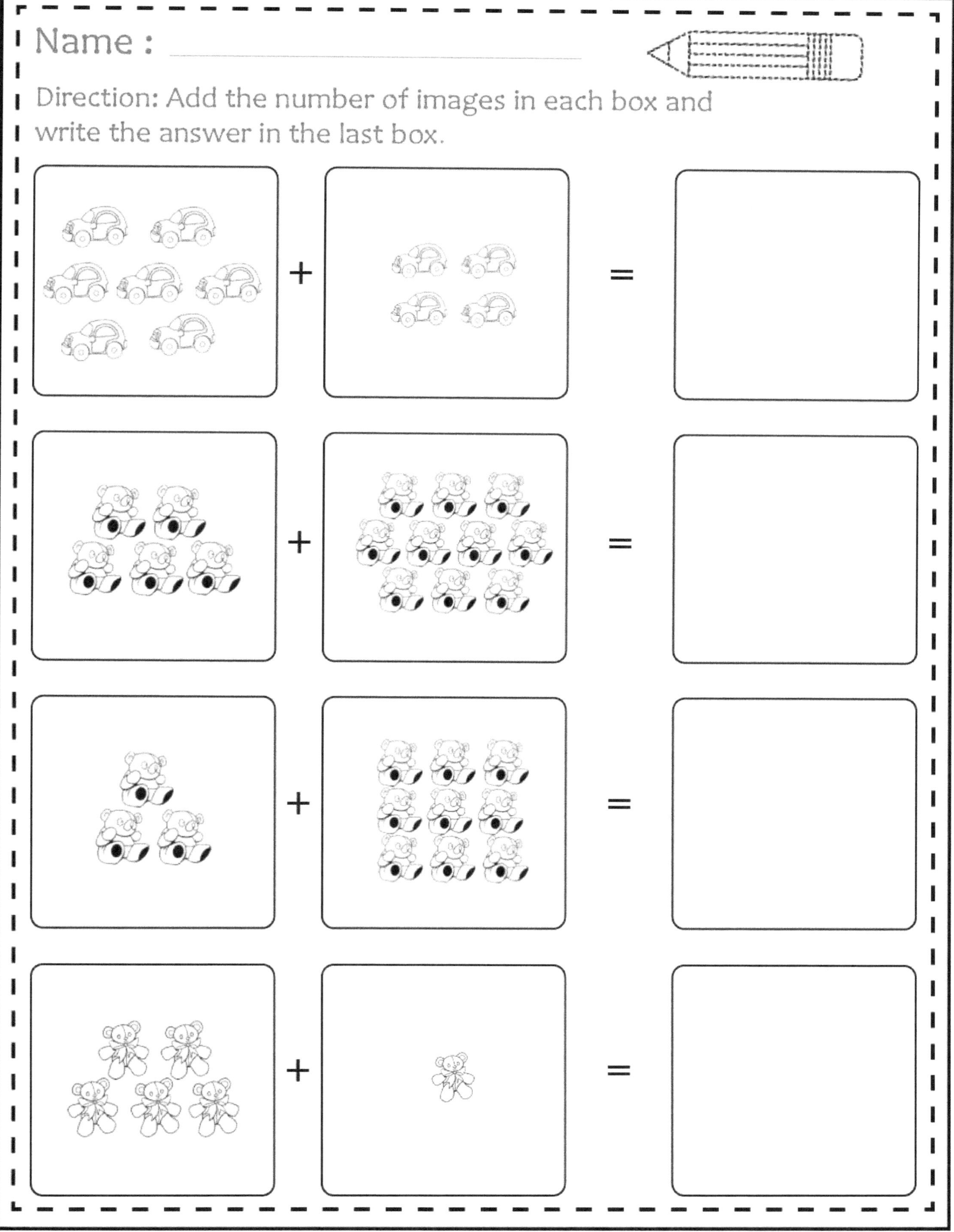

Name : _______________________

Addition Worksheets

3
+ 7

Answer

3
+ 1

Answer

6
+ 2

Answer

1
+ 3

Answer

4
+ 3

Answer

6
+ 8

Answer

Addition Worksheets

18		18		20
+	7	+	6	+	16

18
+ 7

18
+ 6

20
+ 16

16
+ 19

18
+ 13

17
+ 5

8
+ 6

6
+ 5

15
+ 18

Direction: Add the number of images in each box and write the answer in the last box.

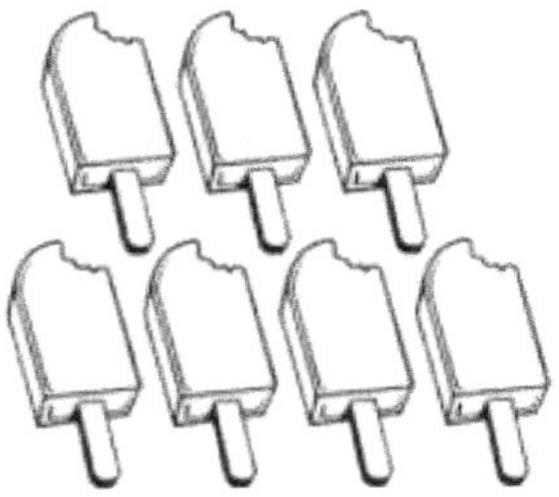

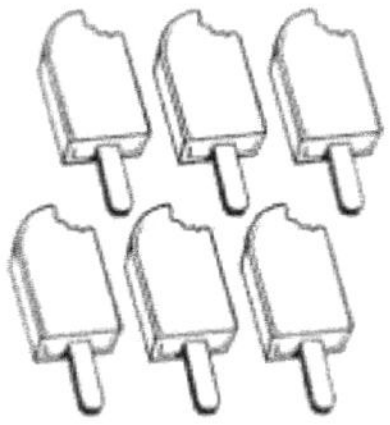

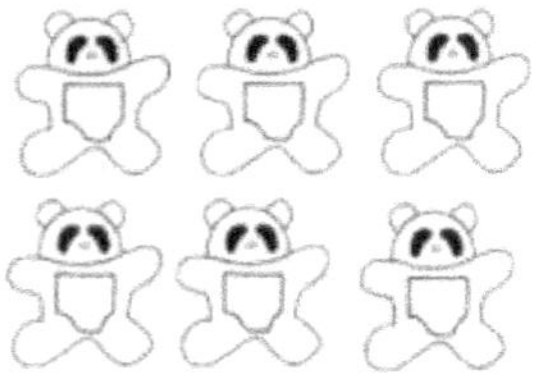

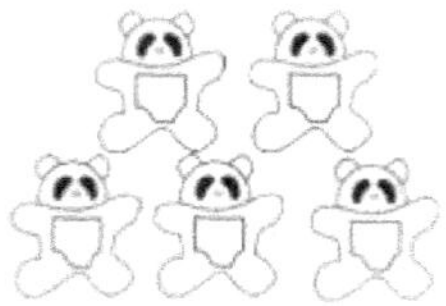

Addition Worksheets

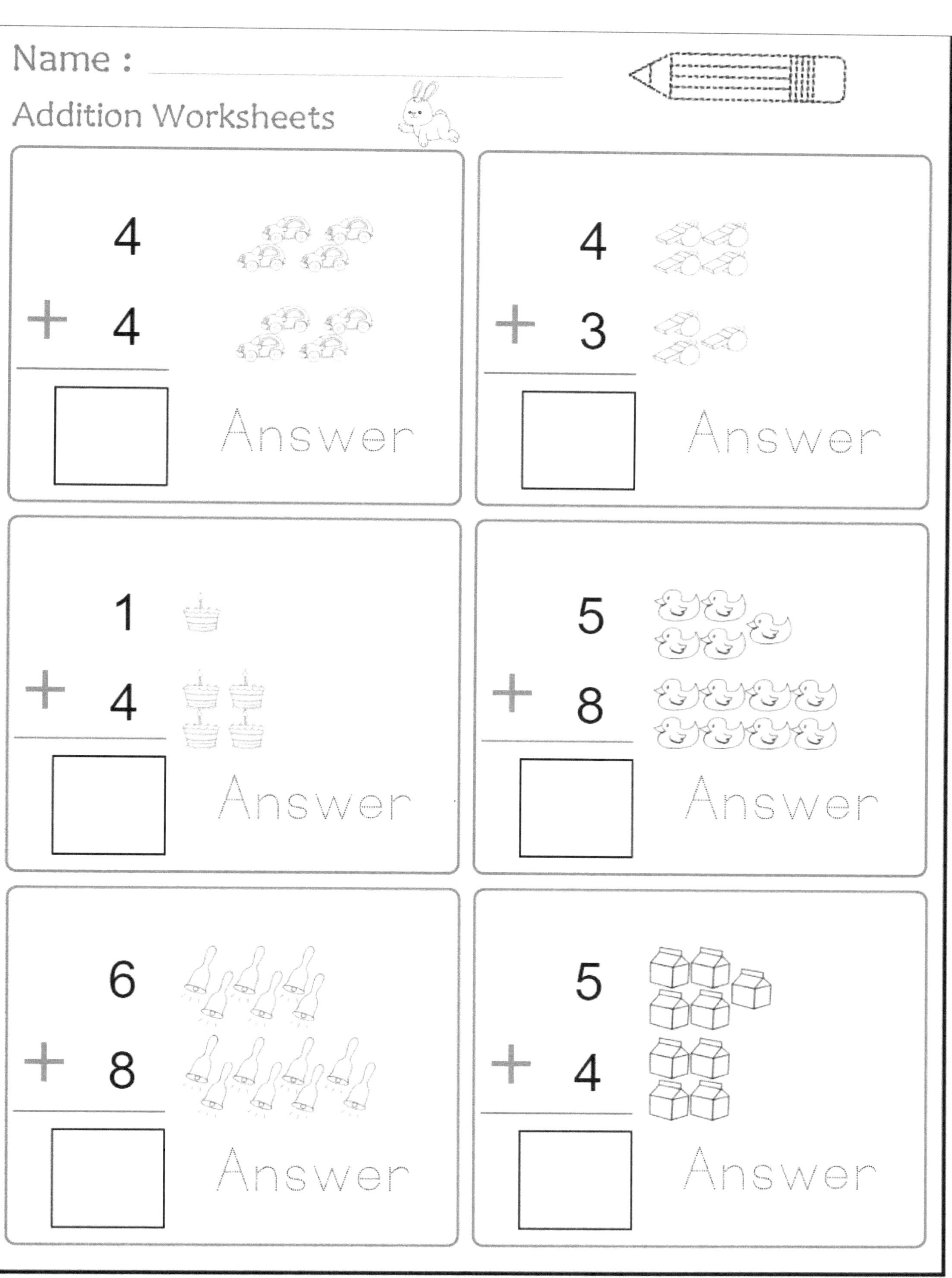

Addition Worksheets

6 + 1	4 + 20	20 + 16
13 + 14	12 + 9	12 + 20
16 + 4	12 + 1	19 + 11

Name : _______________________

Direction: Add the number of images in each box and write the answer in the last box.

Addition Worksheets

1
+ 9

Answer

2
+ 1

Answer

4
+ 8

Answer

3
+ 4

Answer

6
+ 3

Answer

3
+ 1

Answer

Addition Worksheets

9 + 9	4 + 3	12 + 14
20 + 19	3 + 10	16 + 2
12 + 12	12 + 20	13 + 15

Name : _______________________

Direction: Add the number of images in each box and
write the answer in the last box.

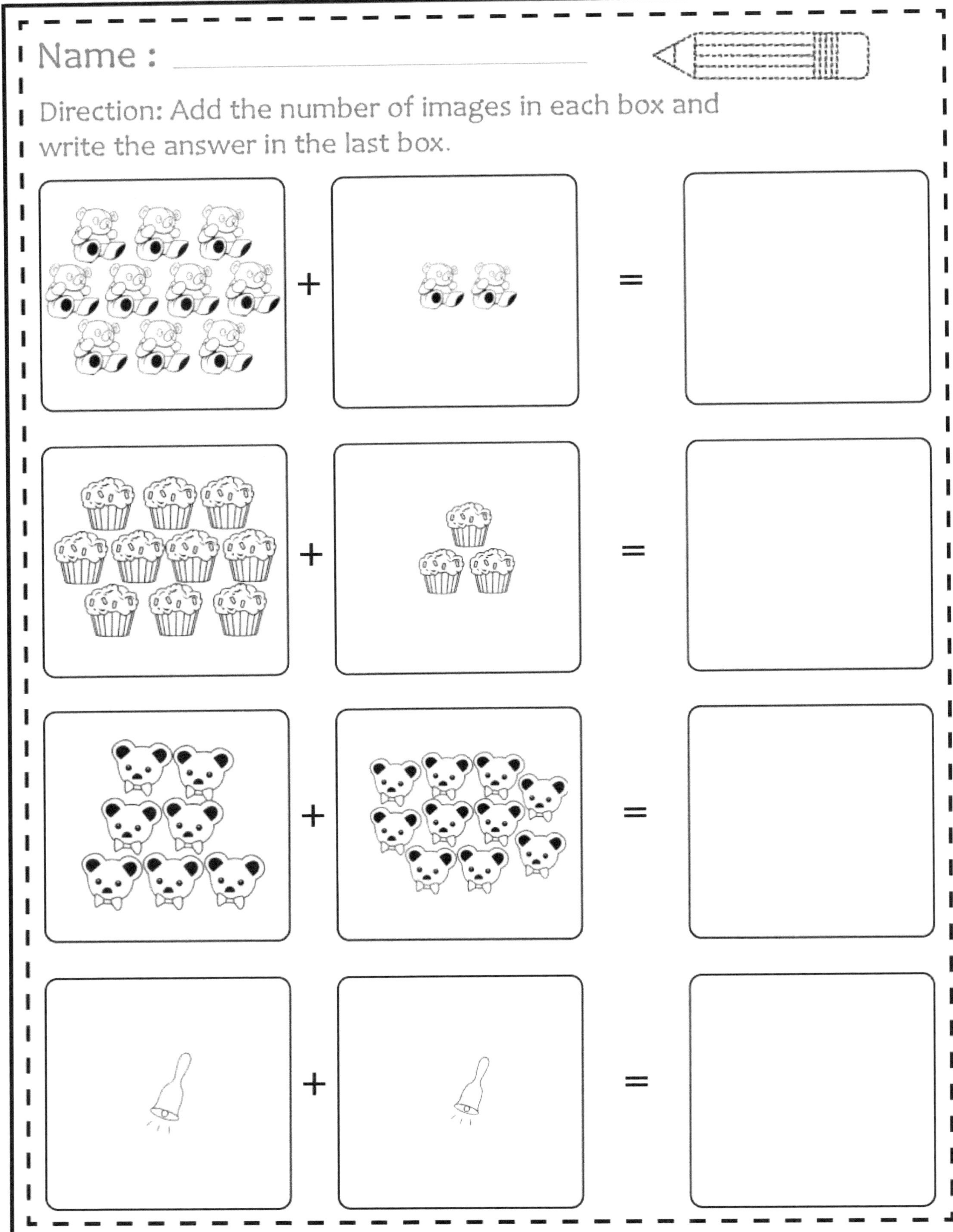

Addition Worksheets

1
+ 9

☐ Answer

2
+ 2

☐ Answer

3
+ 2

☐ Answer

6
+ 3

☐ Answer

1
+ 1

☐ Answer

3
+ 4

☐ Answer

Addition Worksheets

2 + 16	10 + 17	16 + 15
12 + 15	7 + 1	20 + 14
12 + 11	10 + 2	10 + 17

Name : _______________________

Direction: Add the number of images in each box and write the answer in the last box.

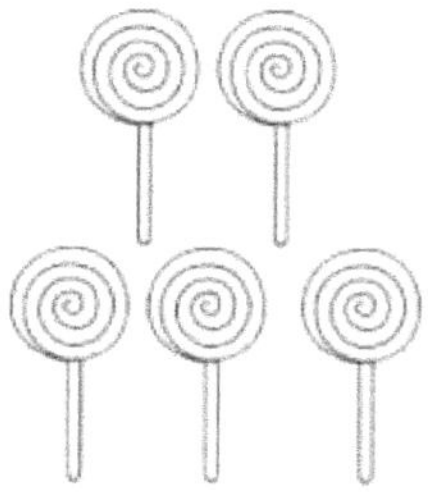

Name : _______________________

Addition Worksheets

4
+ 9

Answer

2
+ 4

Answer

3
+ 1

Answer

3
+ 10

Answer

1
+ 9

Answer

1
+ 1

Answer

2 + 18	17 + 12	14 + 9
10 + 7	11 + 16	4 + 13
19 + 7	13 + 2	11 + 12

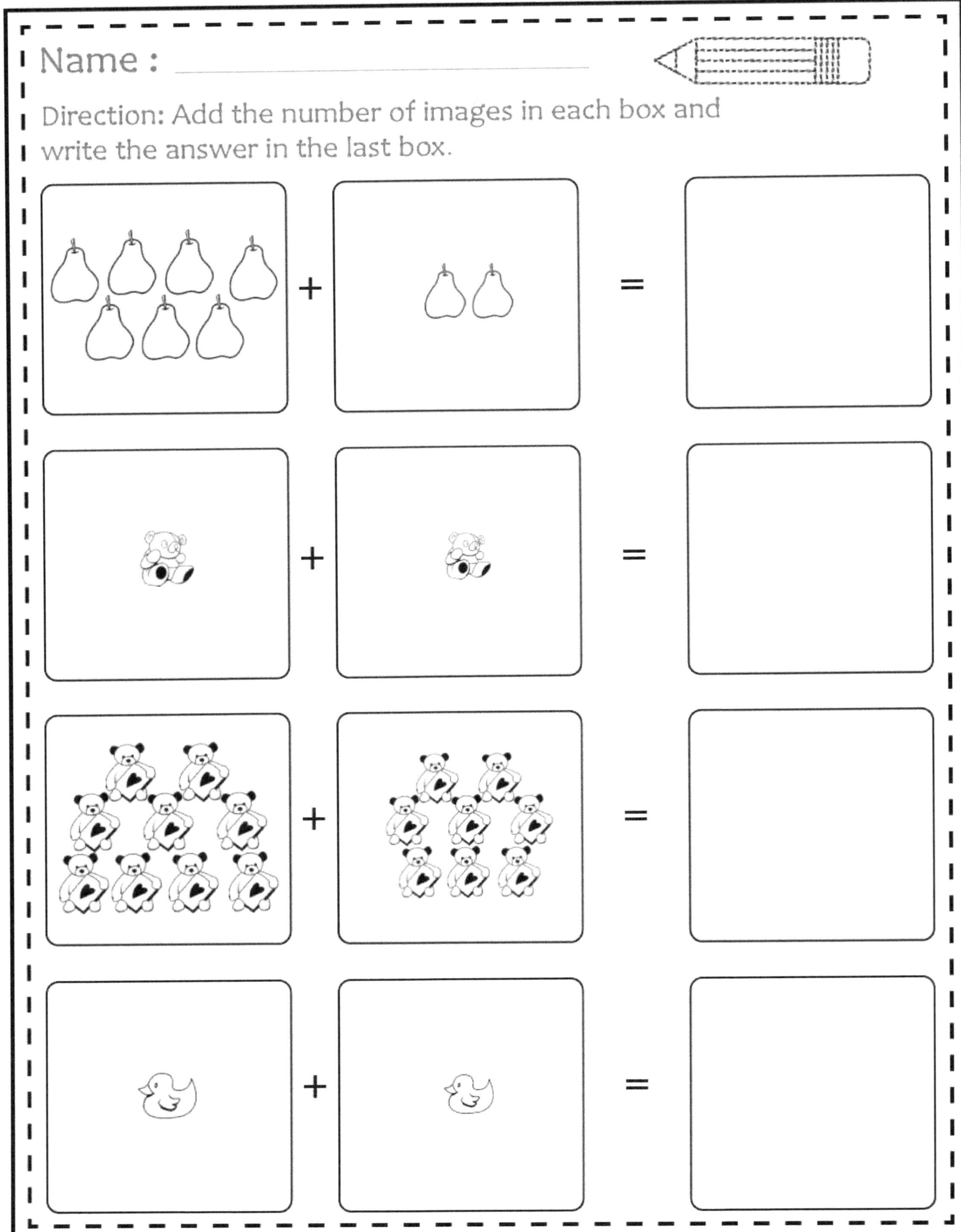

Name :
Direction: Add the number of images in each box and
write the answer in the last box.
+
=
+
=
+
=
+
=

Name :
Addition Worksheets

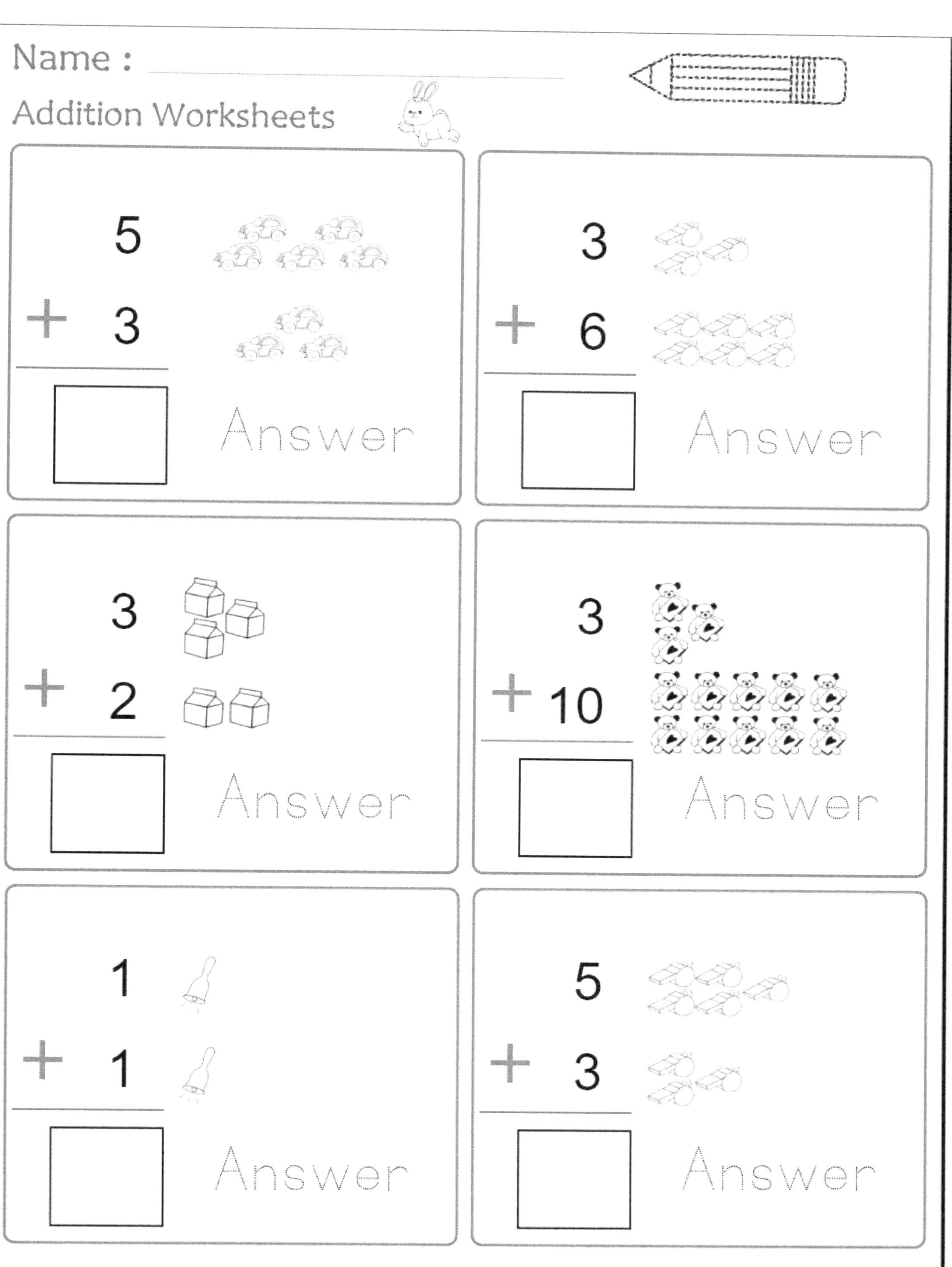

5
+ 3
Answer

3
+ 6
Answer

3
+ 2
Answer

3
+ 10
Answer

1
+ 1
Answer

5
+ 3
Answer

Addition Worksheets

5 + 19	6 + 4	5 + 9
20 + 7	11 + 1	16 + 8
5 + 8	10 + 7	12 + 2

Name : _______________

Direction: Add the number of images in each box and
write the answer in the last box.

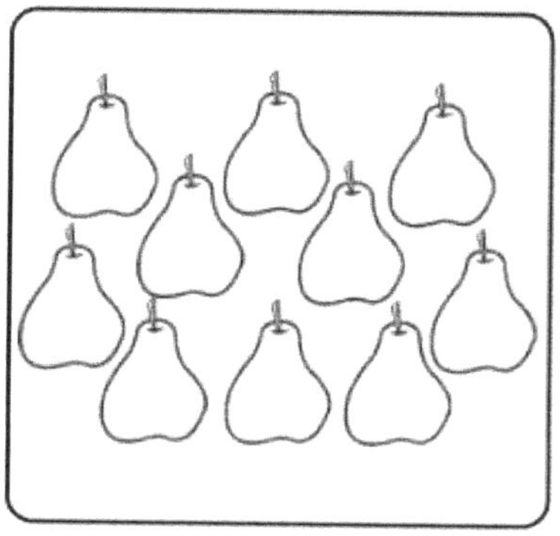

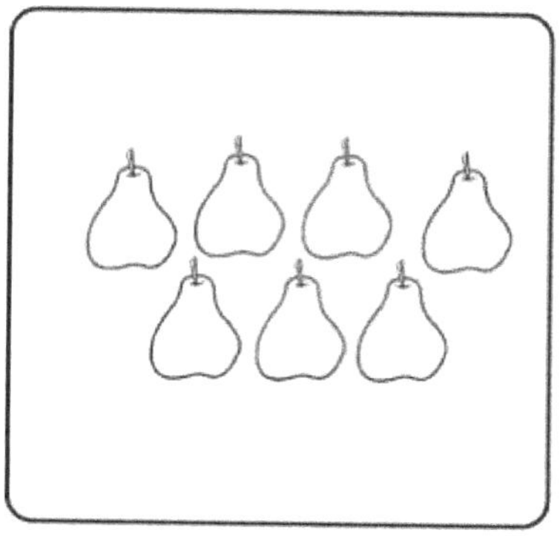

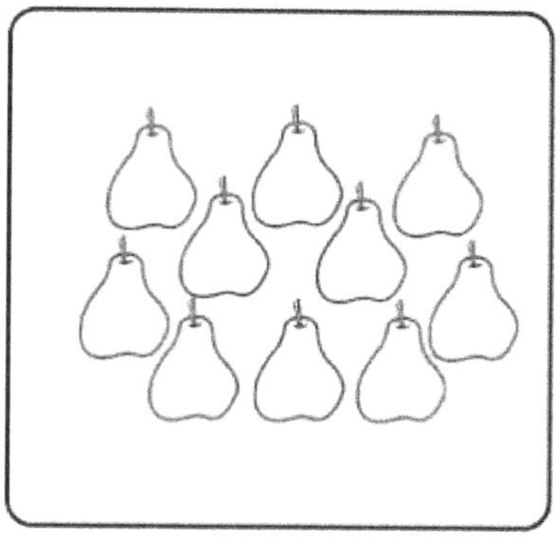

Addition Worksheets

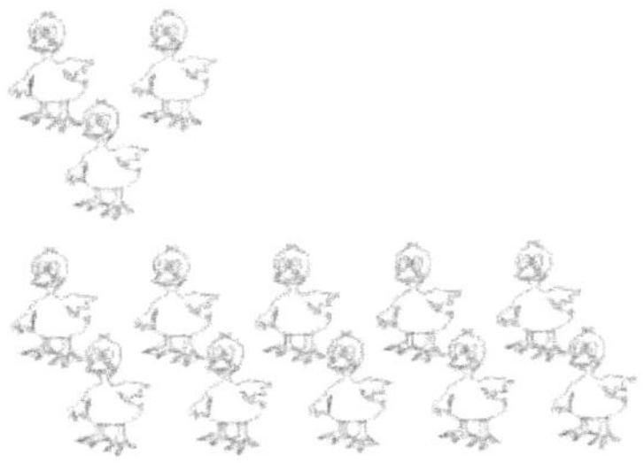

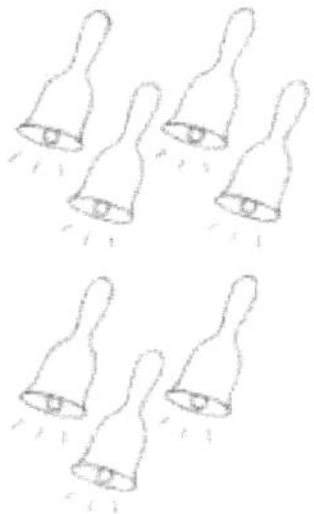

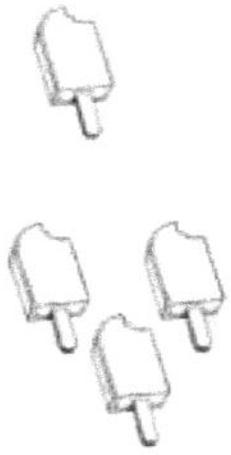

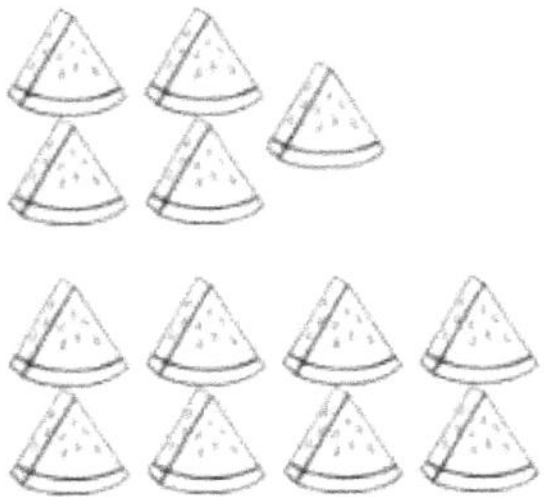

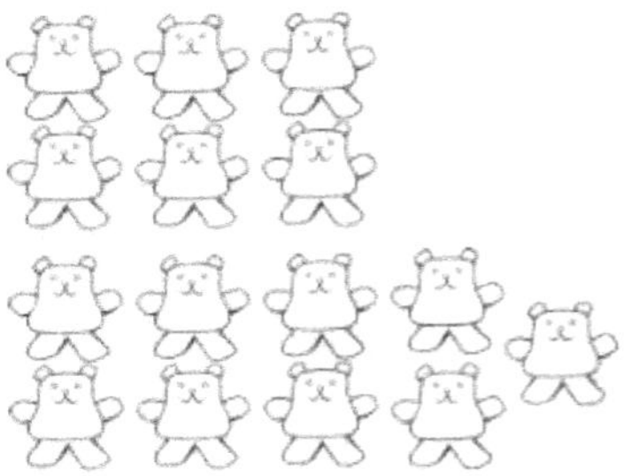

Addition Worksheets

20 + 8	1 + 3

8
+ 3

3
+ 6

20
+ 7

1
+ 7

5
+ 4

15
+ 7

14
+ 11

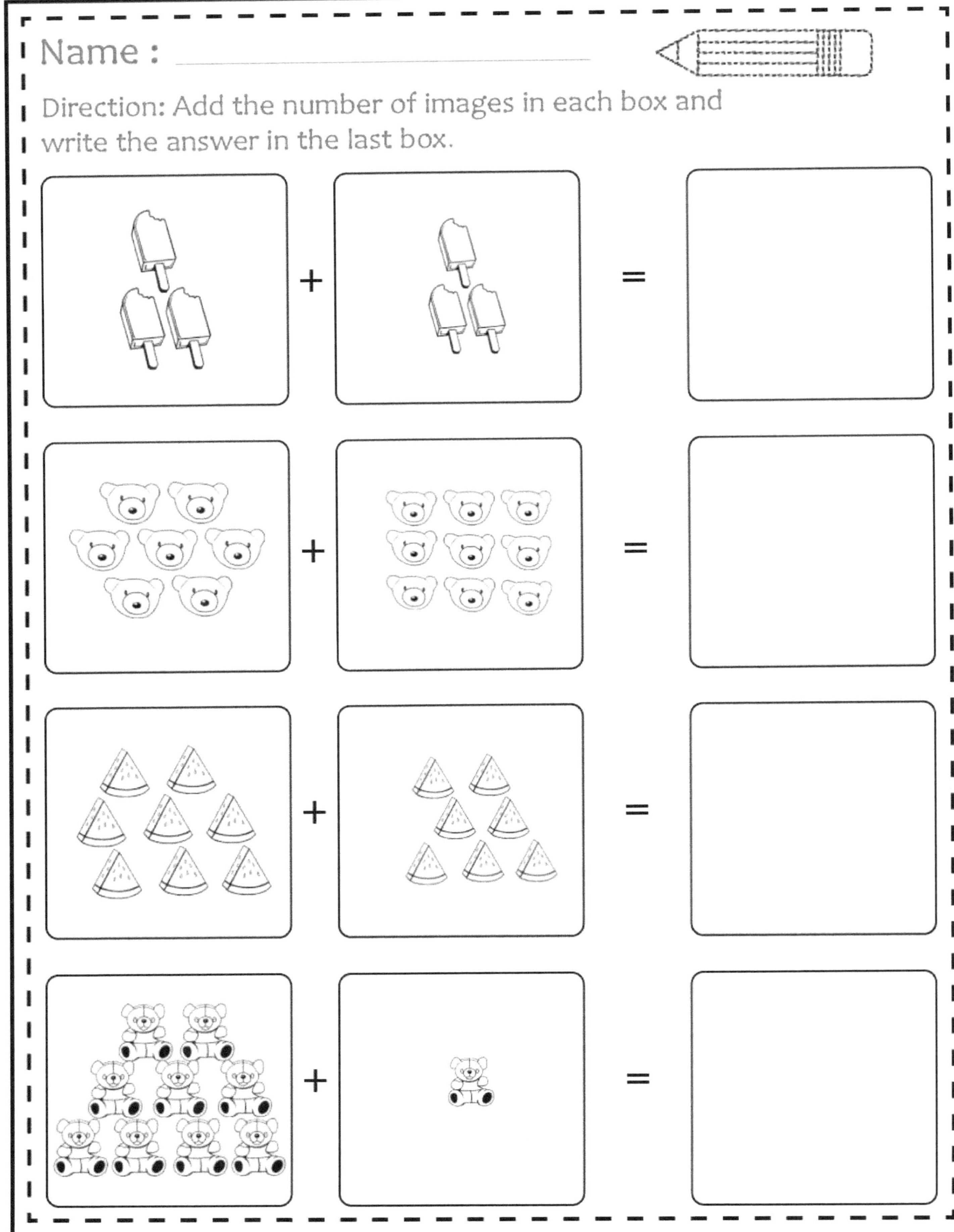

Name :
Direction: Add the number of images in each box and
write the answer in the last box.
+
=
+
=
+
=
+
=

Addition Worksheets

4
+ 4

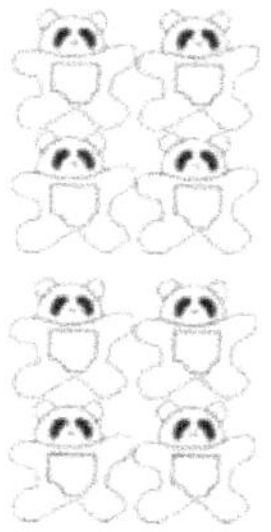

Answer

3
+ 3

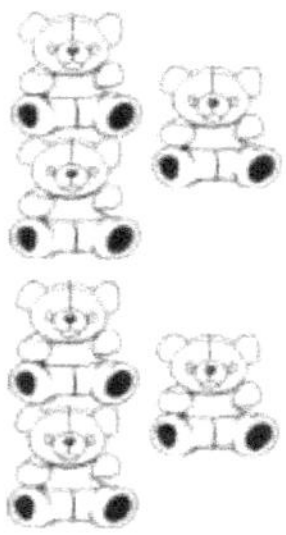

Answer

6
+ 7

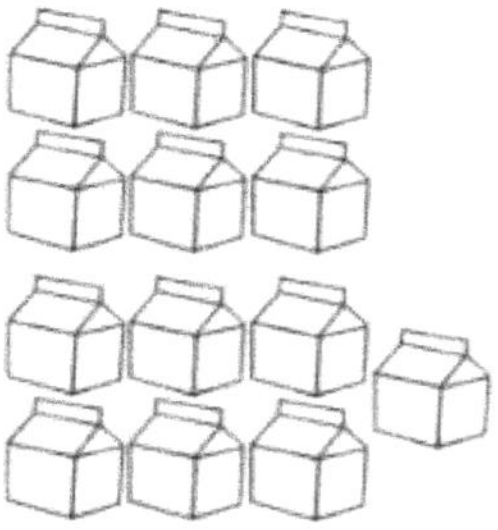

Answer

2
+ 1

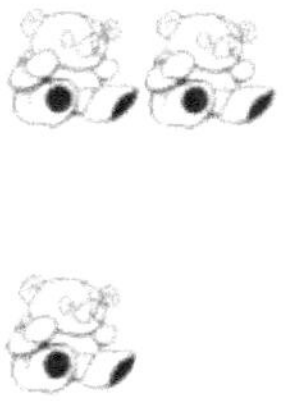

Answer

1
+ 2

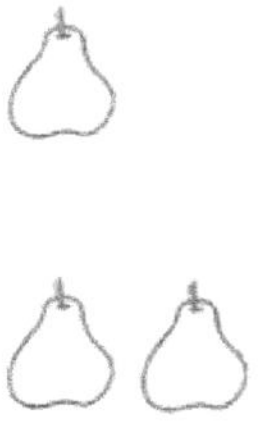

Answer

4
+ 2

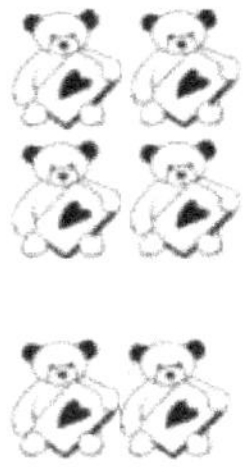

Answer

Addition Worksheets

$$12 + 14 = \square$$

$$20 + 11 = \square$$

$$11 + 12 = \square$$

$$19 + 18 = \square$$

$$2 + 8 = \square$$

$$20 + 14 = \square$$

$$9 + 5 = \square$$

$$14 + 17 = \square$$

$$1 + 13 = \square$$

Name : ___________________________

Direction: Add the number of images in each box and
write the answer in the last box.

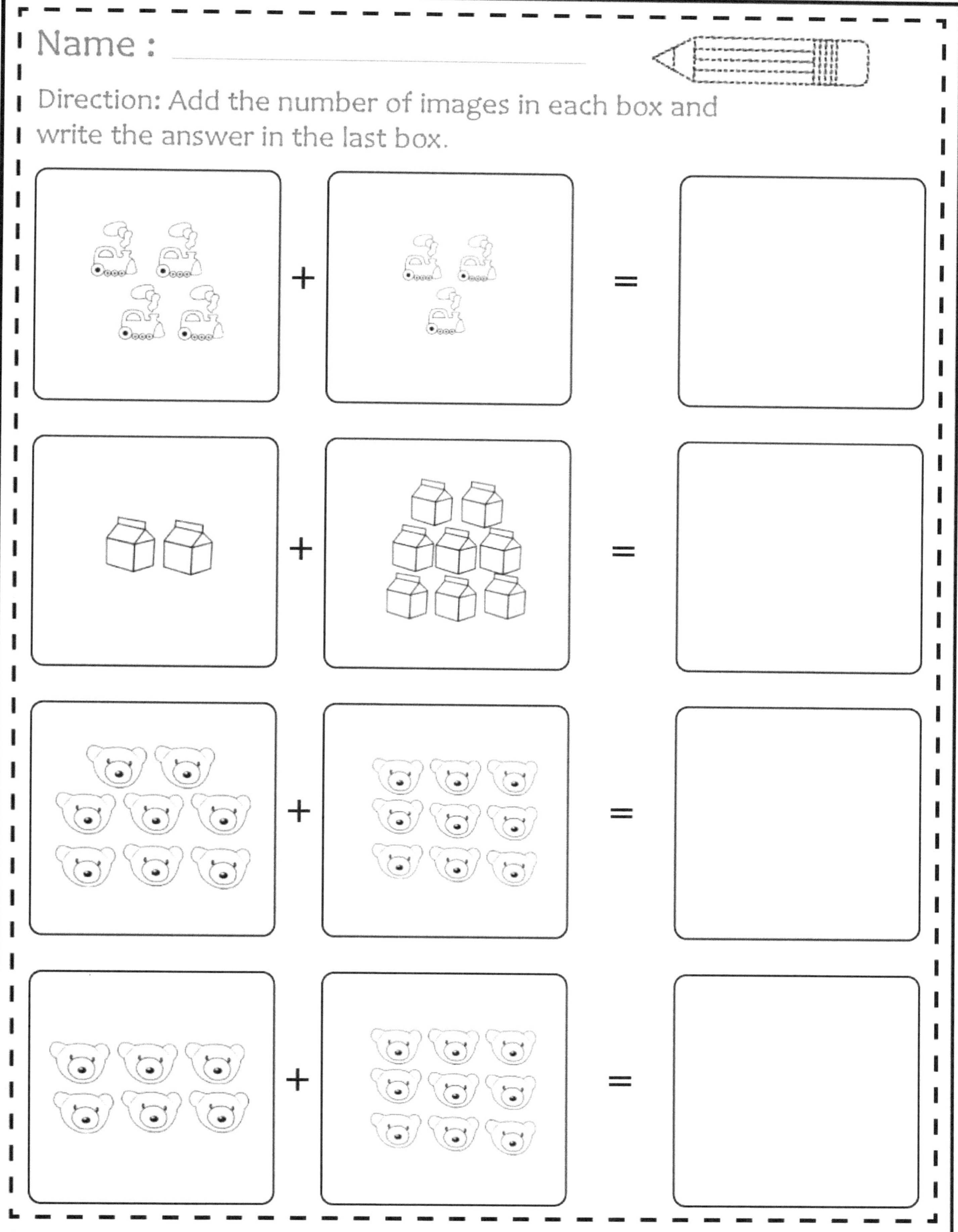

5
+ 10
Answer

4
+ 3
Answer

1
+ 3
Answer

5
+ 3
Answer

1
+ 10
Answer

2
+ 6
Answer

Addition Worksheets

5 + 18	7 + 1	10 + 5
8 + 20	5 + 8	17 + 20
1 + 10	4 + 16	8 + 14

Name : _______________________

Direction: Add the number of images in each box and
write the answer in the last box.

+    =

+    =

+    =

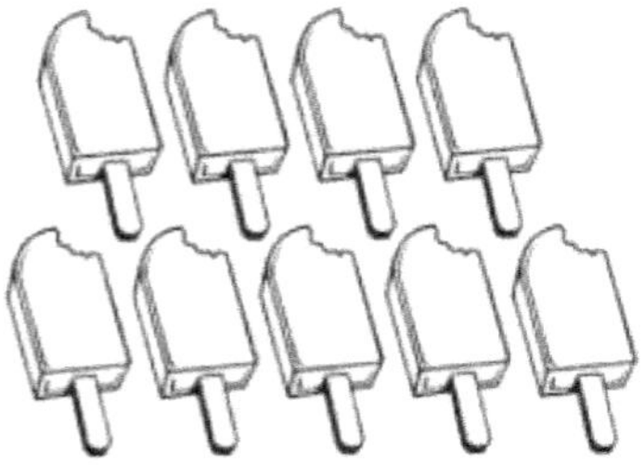

+ 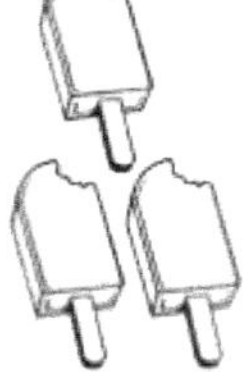   =

Name : ________________

Addition Worksheets

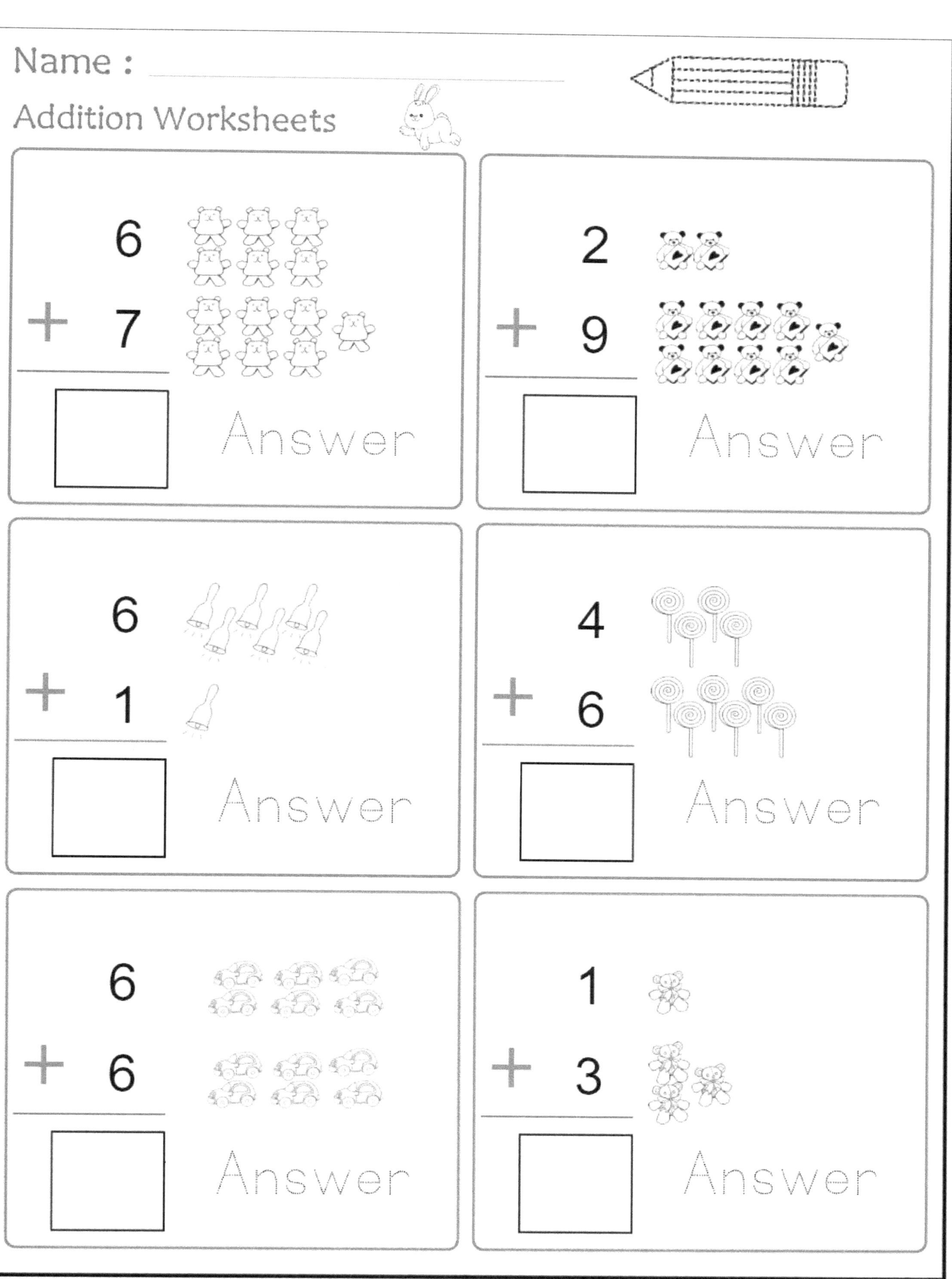

| 8 | 14 | 14 |
| + 2 | + 6 | + 18 |

| 11 | 14 | 17 |
| + 17 | + 7 | + 16 |

| 13 | 5 | 6 |
| + 20 | + 14 | + 13 |

Direction: Add the number of images in each box and write the answer in the last box.

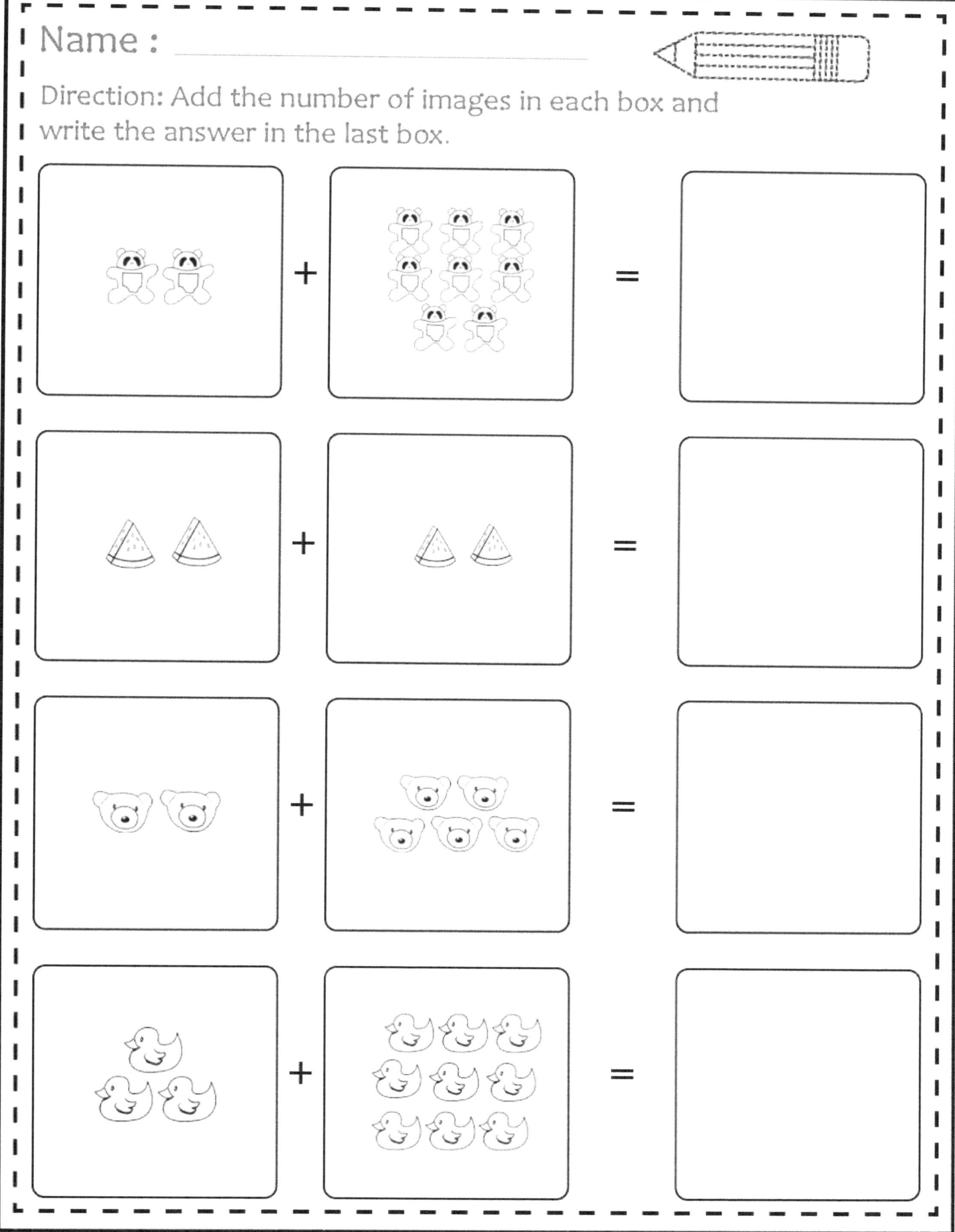

Addition Worksheets

4
+ 7

Answer

6
+ 6

Answer

3
+ 5

Answer

5
+ 4

Answer

3
+ 2

Answer

4
+ 2

Answer

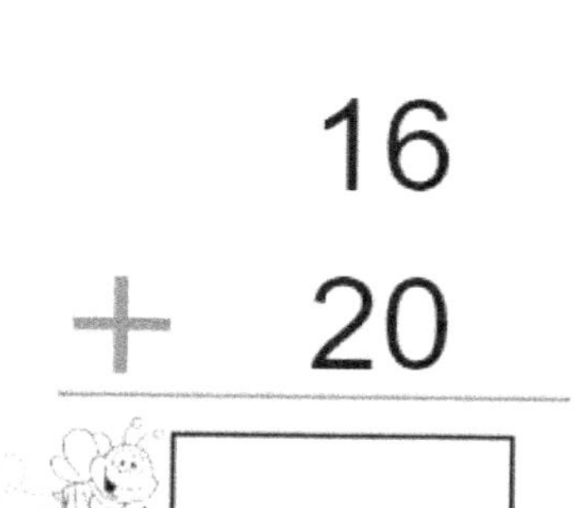

16
+ 20

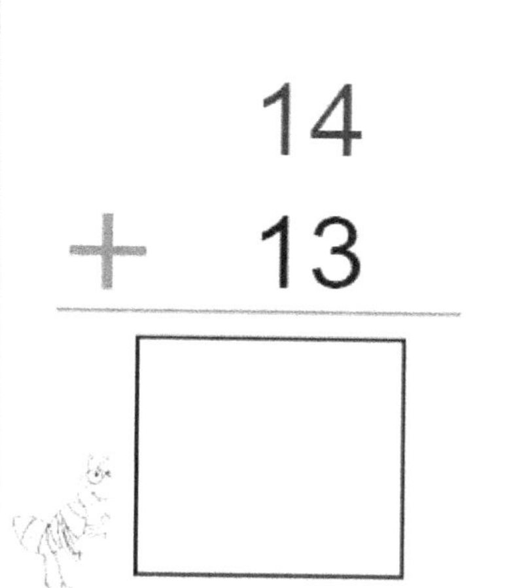

14
+ 13

2
+ 1

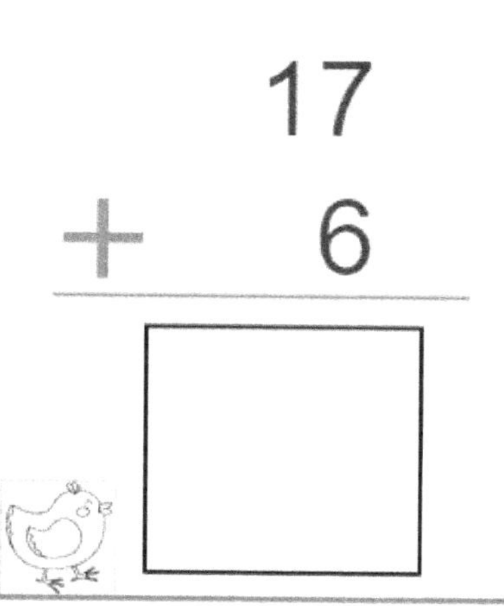

17
+ 6

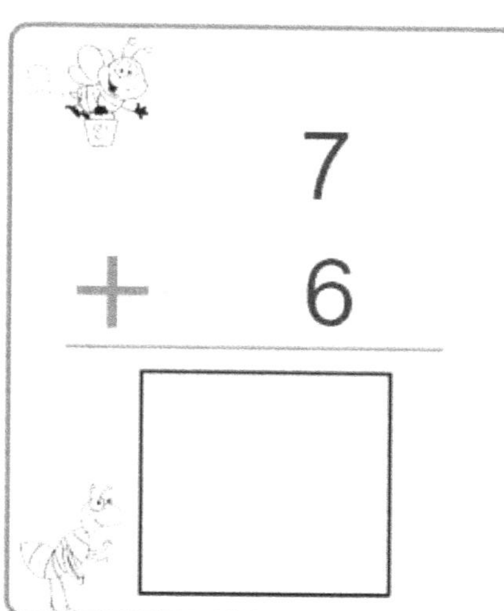

7
+ 6

5
+ 19

1
+ 10

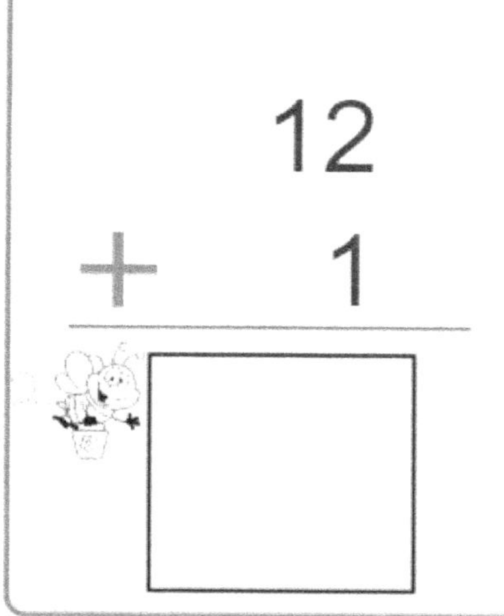

12
+ 1

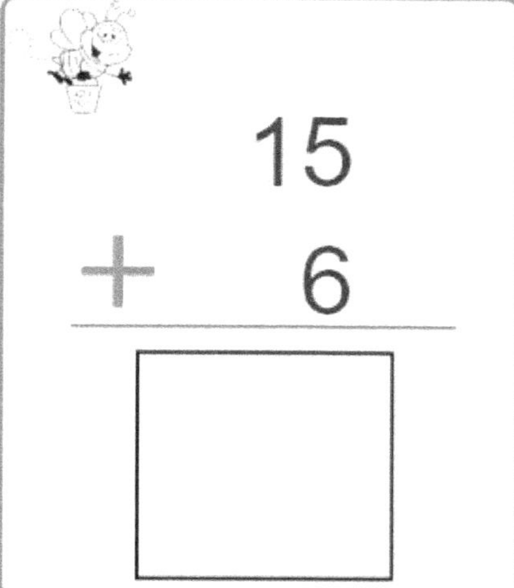

15
+ 6

Direction: Add the number of images in each box and write the answer in the last box.

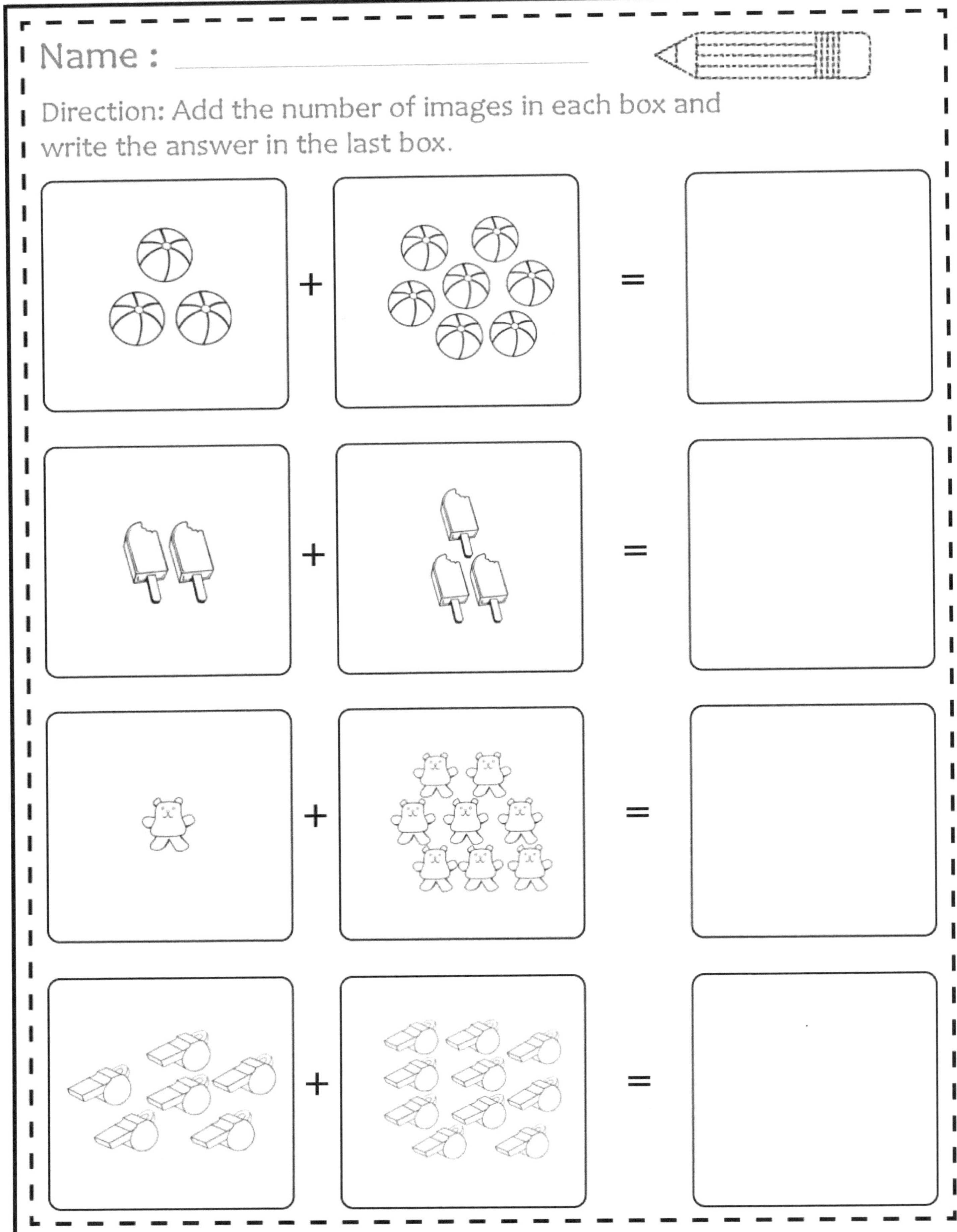

Name :
Addition Worksheets

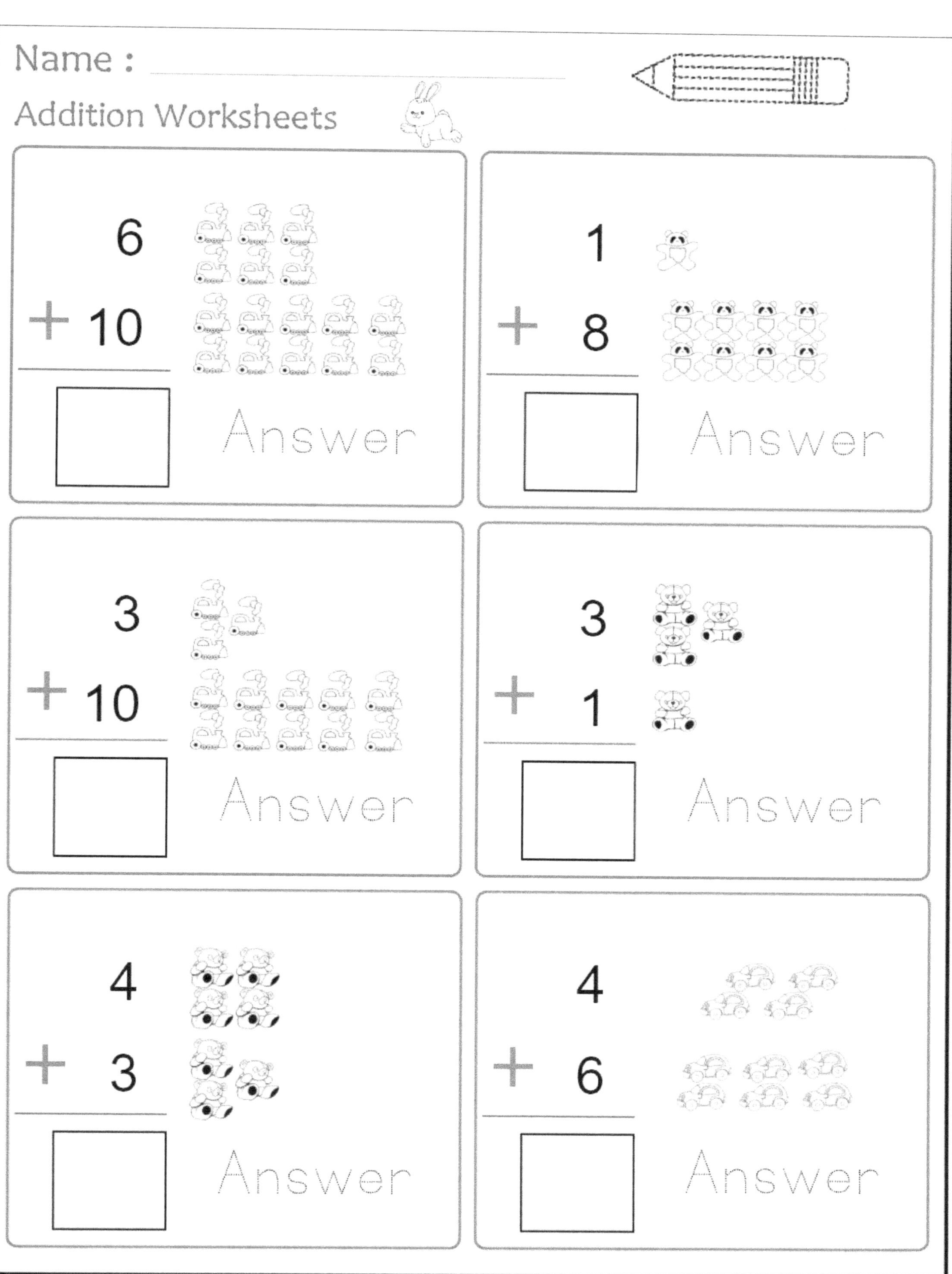

6
+ 10
Answer

1
+ 8
Answer

3
+ 10
Answer

3
+ 1
Answer

4
+ 3
Answer

4
+ 6
Answer

Addition Worksheets

1
+ 11

9
+ 8

13
+ 19

10
+ 6

20
+ 19

6
+ 2

18
+ 6

18
+ 20

9
+ 7

Name : ___________________

Direction: Add the number of images in each box and write the answer in the last box.

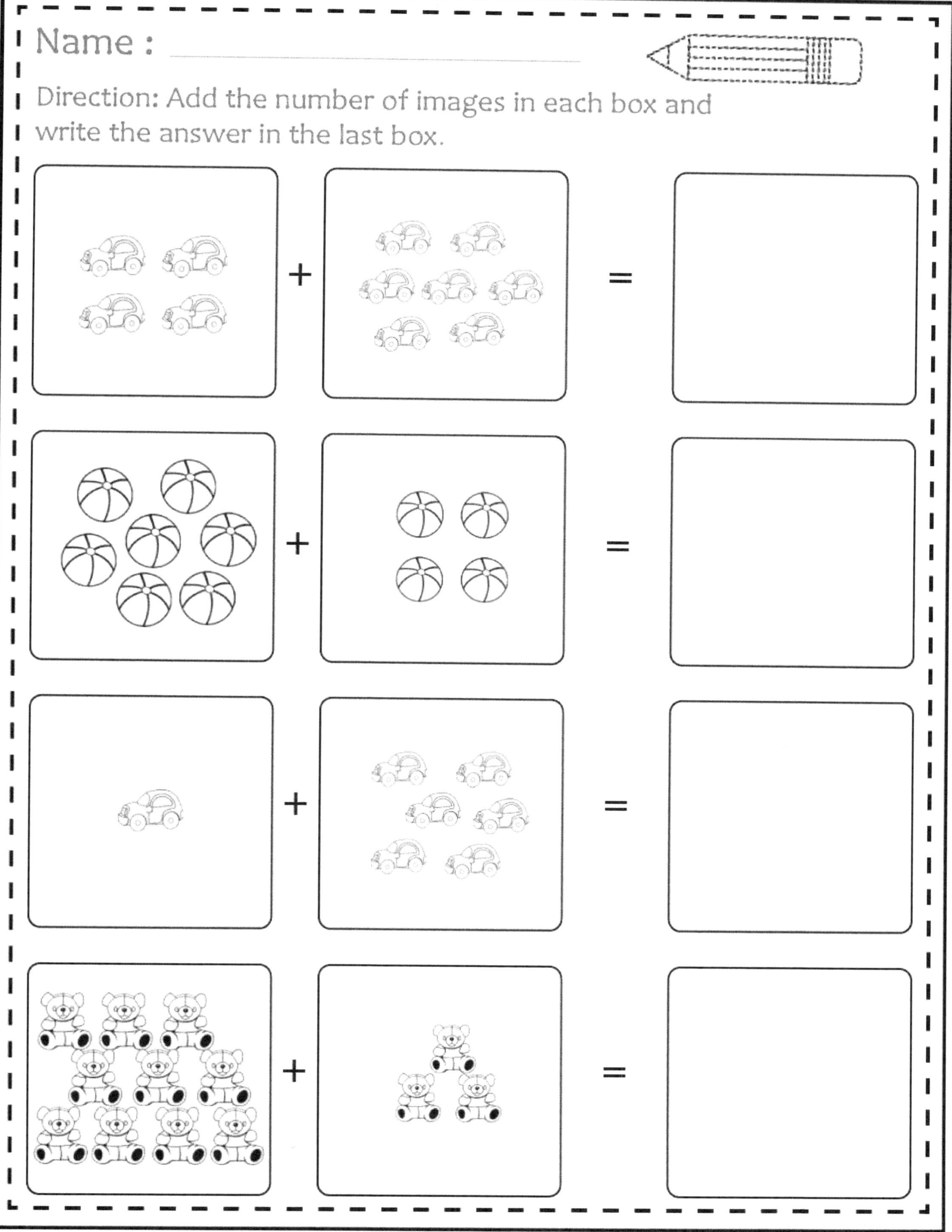

Addition Worksheets

4
+ 4
[   ] Answer

3
+ 4
[   ] Answer

3
+ 8
[   ] Answer

3
+ 8
[   ] Answer

3
+ 4
[   ] Answer

4
+ 7
[   ] Answer

Addition Worksheets

20
+ 16

6
+ 4

1
+ 1

11
+ 1

6
+ 6

2
+ 19

17
+ 2

14
+ 8

6
+ 1

Name : _______________________________

Direction: Add the number of images in each box and
write the answer in the last box.

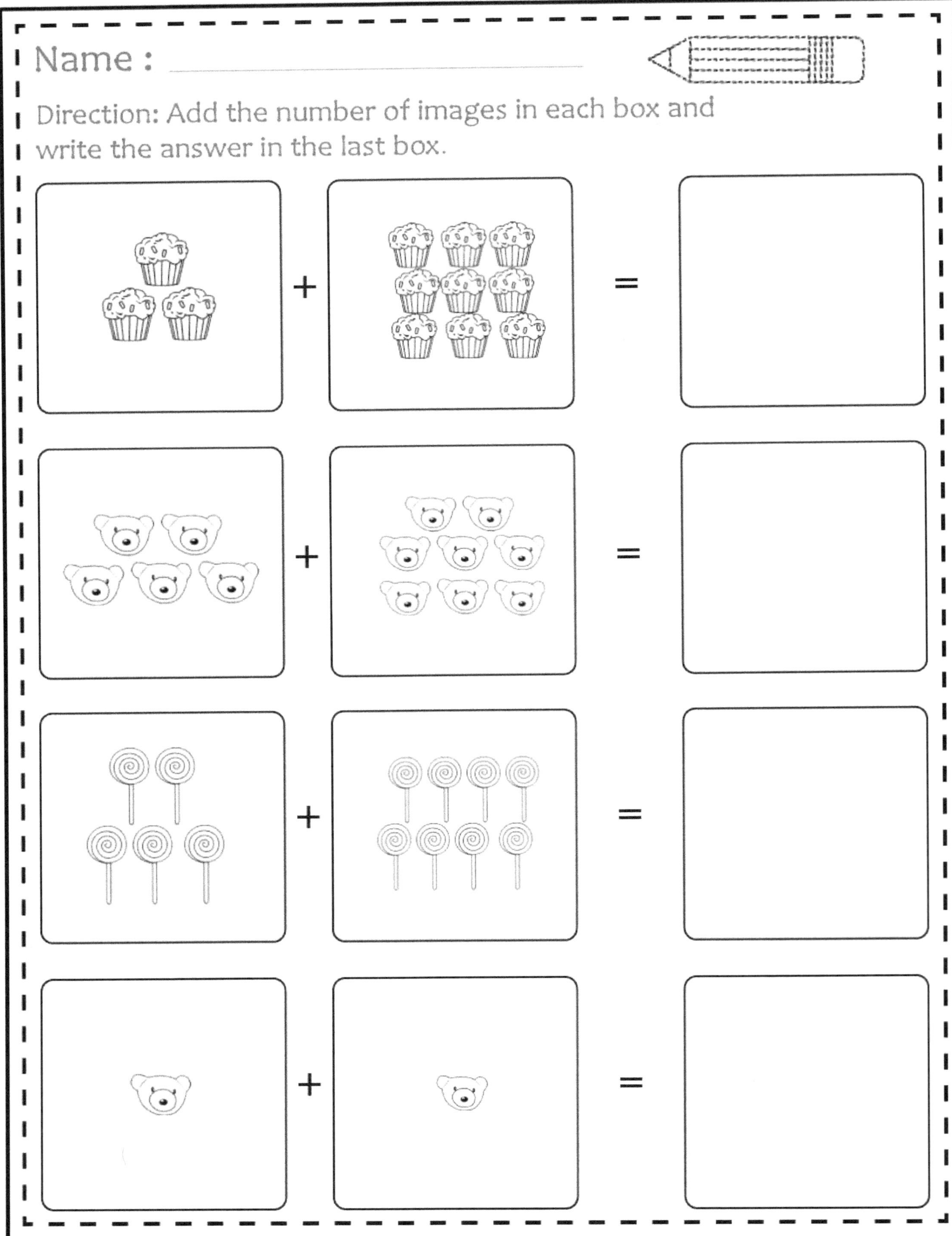

Name :
Addition Worksheets

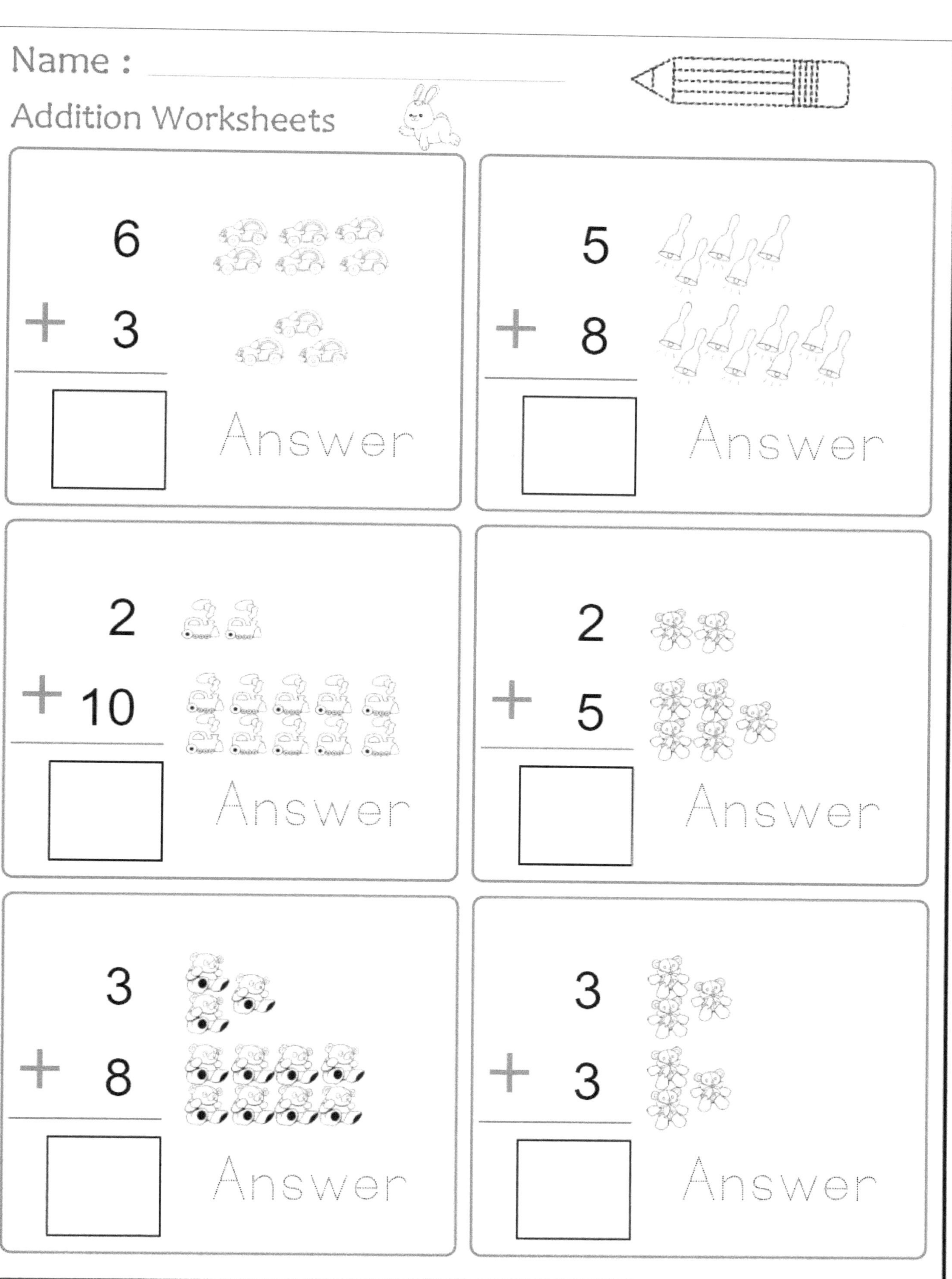

6
+ 3
Answer

5
+ 8
Answer

2
+ 10
Answer

2
+ 5
Answer

3
+ 8
Answer

3
+ 3
Answer

Addition Worksheets

14 + 11	12 + 15	6 + 6
14 + 20	18 + 12	7 + 8
15 + 12	4 + 17	19 + 8

Name :

Direction: Add the number of images in each box and
write the answer in the last box.

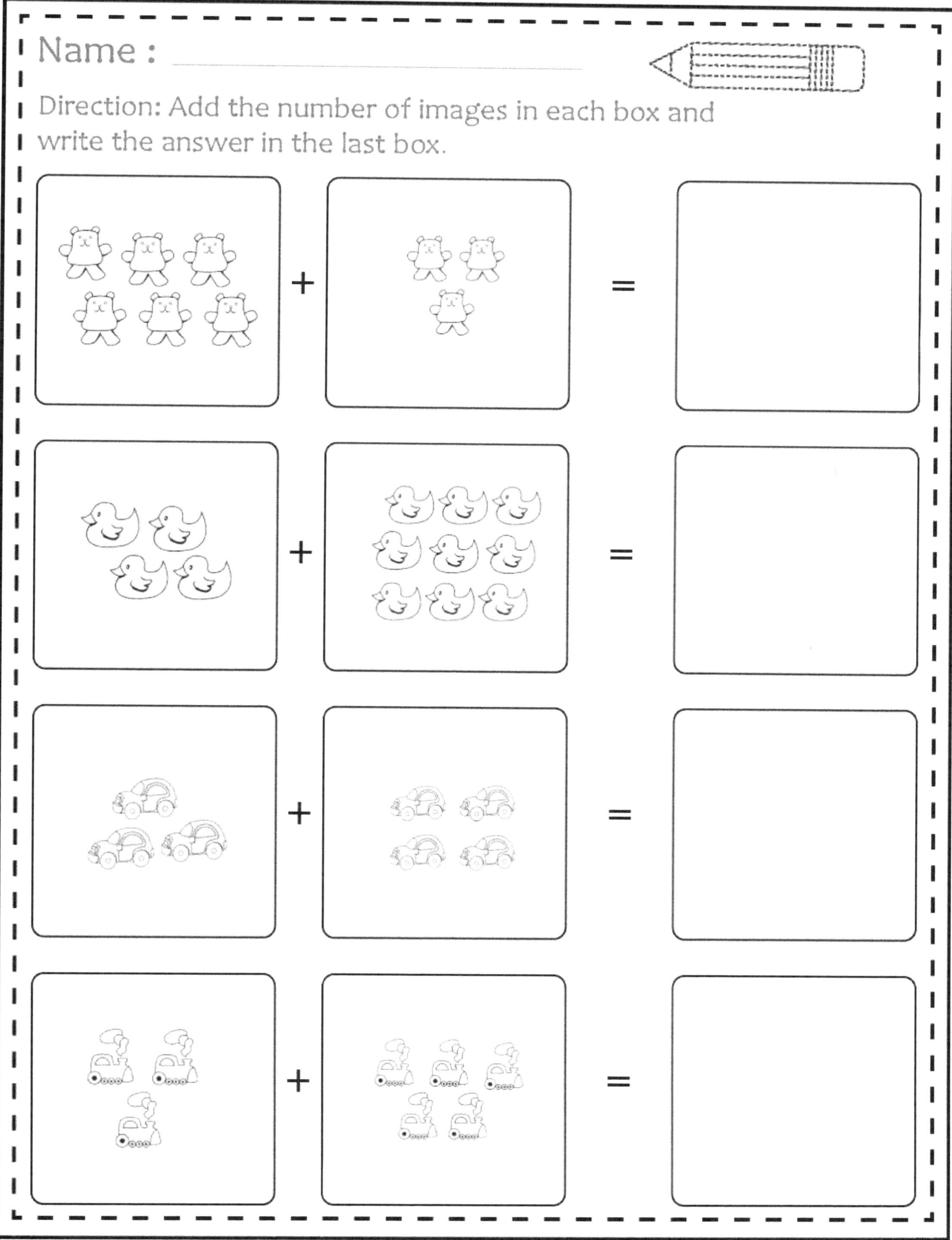

Name :
Addition Worksheets

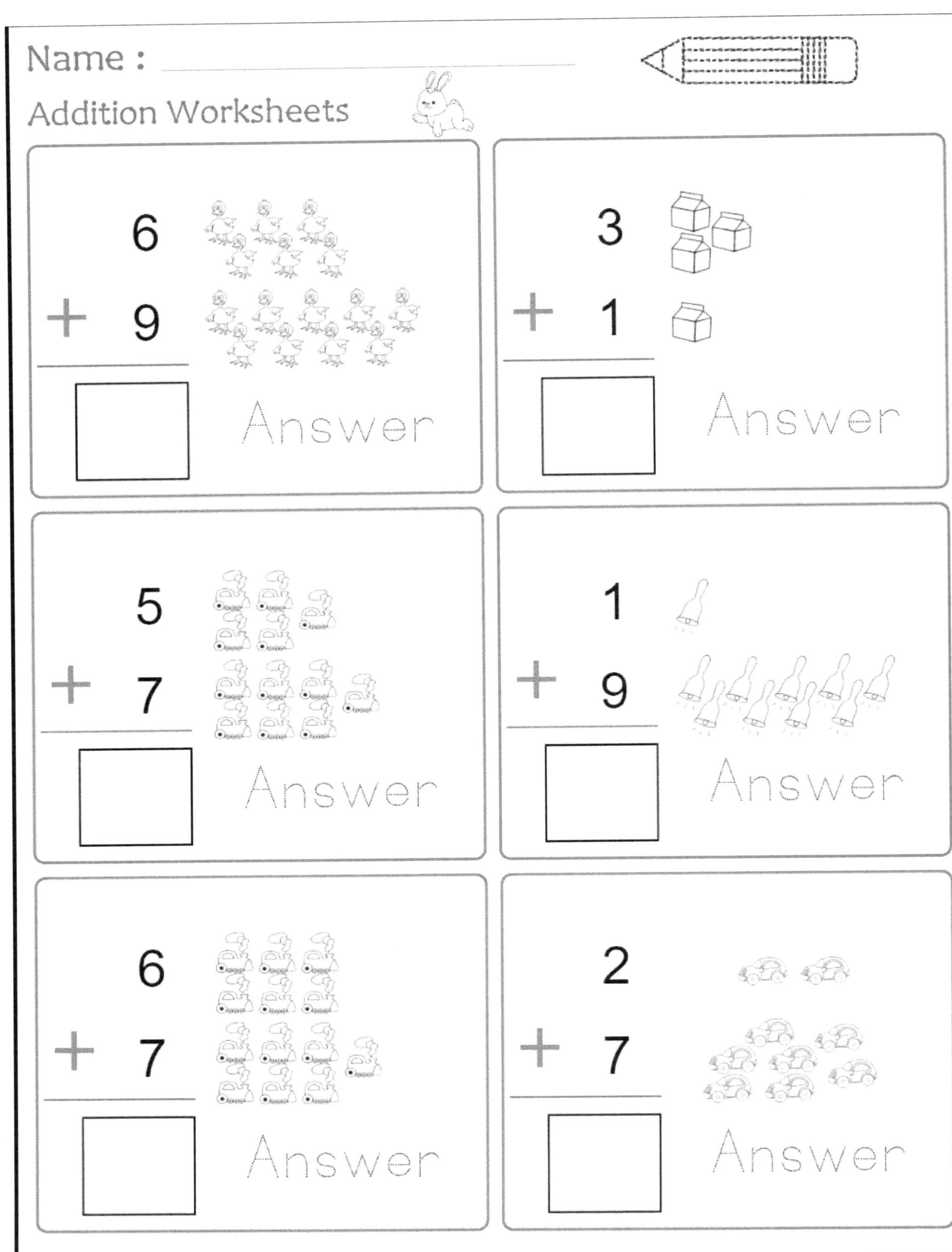

6
+ 9
Answer

3
+ 1
Answer

5
+ 7
Answer

1
+ 9
Answer

6
+ 7
Answer

2
+ 7
Answer

Addition Worksheets

14 + 20	8 + 11	14 + 17
18 + 1	12 + 1	19 + 15
3 + 6	1 + 16	12 + 17

Name : ________________

Direction: Add the number of images in each box and write the answer in the last box.

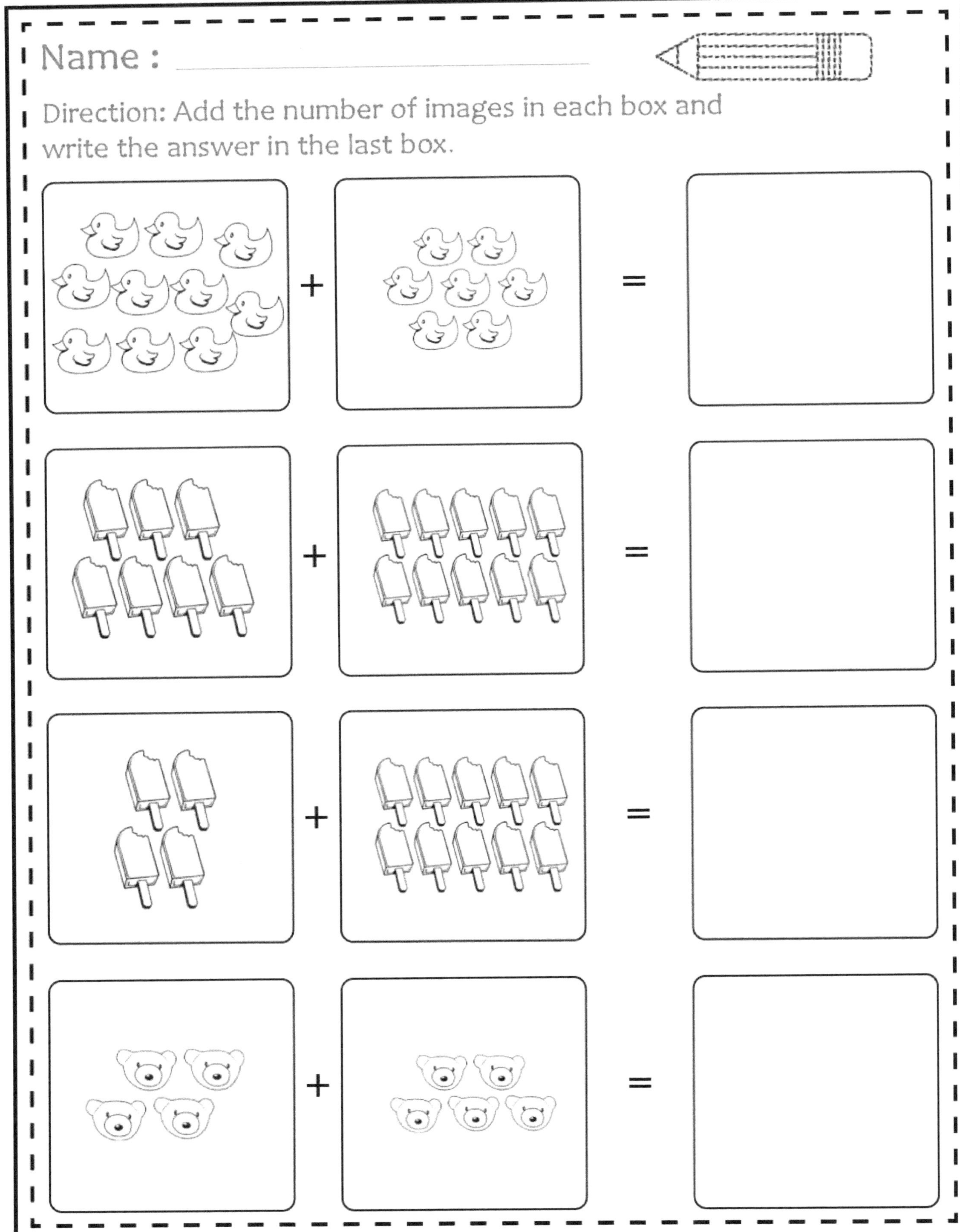

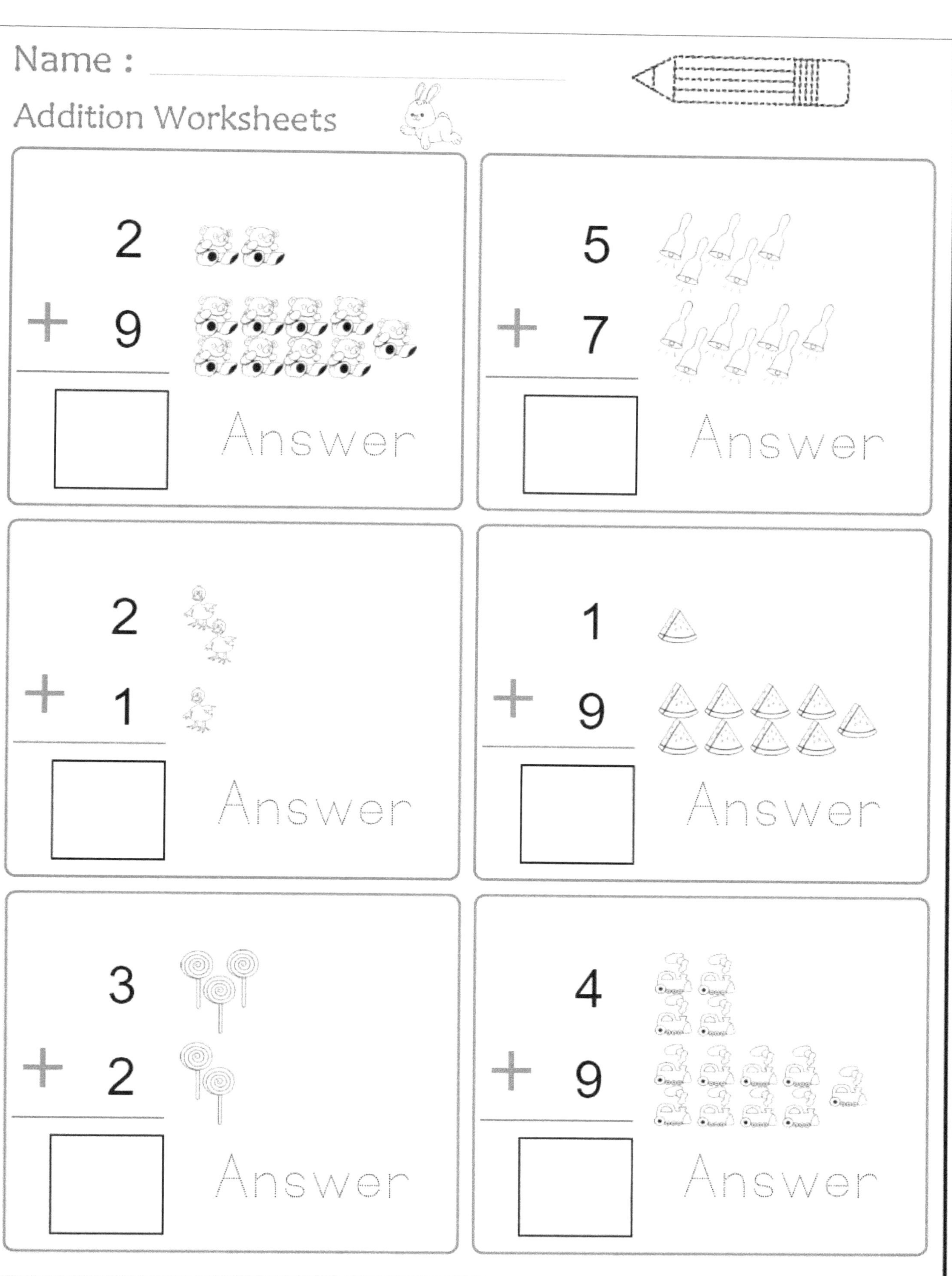

Name :
Addition Worksheets

2
+ 9
Answer

5
+ 7
Answer

2
+ 1
Answer

1
+ 9
Answer

3
+ 2
Answer

4
+ 9
Answer